THE BUSINESS OF SHORT STORIES

WRITING, SUBMITTING, PUBLISHING, AND MARKETING

SHANNON LAWRENCE

WARRIOR MUSE PRESS

Warrior Muse Press

www.thewarriormuse.com

Cover Design © 2021 Jeff Lawrence

Cover Image Stock Illustration Seamless Pattern on the Theme © 2021 Zagory | Deposit Photos

Cover Image Stock Illustration Colorful Paper Note Adhesive Tape © 2021 Vectorism | Deposit Photos

Title Font Uni Sans © 2021 Svetoslave Simon, Fontfabric | 1001 Fonts

Notes Font Gemelli © 1997, 2001 Jason Pagura, Cuttlefish | 1001 Fonts

Author Photo © 2015 Jared Hagan

ISBN: 978-1-7320314-5-6

CONTENTS

PART ONE
INTRODUCTION

INTRODUCTION

During my time learning how to submit short stories and make it into a business, I repeatedly found that there were plenty of books on how to write a short story, but none on what to do with it after I'd written it. There was nothing about how to find markets, how to craft a cover letter, what editors wanted outside of their submission guidelines, and so forth. Because of this, I had to wing it, to learn as I went. Now here I am, with over fifty short stories published. In looking around again recently, I found the same problem existed: a lot of people wanted to tell me how to write a short story, something that had come naturally for me to begin with, but not what to do with it afterward. You know why? Many of the people writing those books are actually novelists who merely dabble in short stories. That's why this book exists now.

This book is intended as a jumping off point for those of you who want to actively submit or publish those gems you've written. While there is a section on writing them, it's brief and meant to give the basics, the dynamics behind the short story. The true intent of this book is to help you become a professional short story author and to grow comfortable with the process faster than you might have otherwise. Hopefully without having to learn the hard way through your mistakes like I did.

I come at this as someone who has a passion for the art of short stories, and who has been working in the field for over a decade. I've learned a lot through my own experiences, but also through speaking to friends who are editors and published authors. In an attempt to learn and improve my craft, I've done significant research on the art and the field. The information I'm presenting in this book is hard won in many cases, but it has all been worth it to continue being an author of short stories. Each new release is a reward in itself, and I'd like others to get to feel how delightful and satisfying it can be. So much of the writing world focuses on novels, but short stories are a viable and satisfying option for those who have no interest in writing a novel.

Short stories have existed for a long time and will continue to exist and even to flourish well into the future. They're an art form separate from novel writing, and my first and favorite love in writing. When writing short, you're forced to be succinct, to boil the vision in your head down to its basic form, while still conveying character, setting, and story arc, and entertaining in the process.

Neil Gaiman said, "Short stories are tiny windows into other worlds and other minds and other dreams. They are journeys you can make to the far side of the universe and still be back in time for dinner."

In addition to Neil Gaiman, other well-known fiction authors who've written short stories include Robert Heinlein, Clive Barker, Ken Liu, Stephen King, N.K. Jemisin, George R.R. Martin, Edgar Allan Poe, Shirley Jackson, Margaret Atwood, Sylvia Moreno-Garcia, Ray Bradbury, Alice Munro, Flannery O'Connor, Stephen Graham Jones, and Mark Twain. There are, of course, many more who've joined this elite club, but there should be at least one recognizable name in this batch. Writing short stories stretches different muscles than longer works, and not everyone who writes one form well can do so with the other. These folks have stood out in both.

If you're coming at this as a novelist who wants to play in the short story world, that's viable, too! The reasons to explore short stories are many and varied. Here are a few:

- Honing your craft. The more you write, the more you learn

and grow. If you're writing one long novel and nothing else in between, you're missing the opportunity to stretch your skills and practice as you go.
- Learning brevity and succinctness.
- It can help when you're being sidetracked by extra characters and storylines. Write a short story about them instead! Then offer it as a reader magnet or submit it for publication.
- Address backstory to get unstuck. This may work out issues AND you'll have something to publish or offer as a reader magnet.
- Bring in extra money while working on a novel.
- Have published short stories to put in a query letter, rather than having no experience to offer.
- Gain exposure, which might draw readers to your novels.
- Instant gratification.

Short stories can also be a lot of fun to write, and they bring many opportunities to their writers that novelists just don't have. Understand that there's nothing standing in the way of only writing short stories. There is absolutely no requirement saying you have to be a novel writer to be a real author. That's not at all true, and you'll see that as the book progresses. There are people who only write short, and who have solid careers based on that skill. My focus has been on short stories for years now, and I've done well for myself based on that. Write what you're interested in, what stokes your passion, and what makes you happy. Don't let others tell you it's supposed to be a different way.

PART TWO
WRITING SHORT STORIES

What to Expect:

- Word count definition
- General rules of short stories (pacing, character, arcs, plot, backstory, conflict, setting, etc.)
- Editing
- Critique groups and beta readers

CHAPTER 1
DEFINING THE SHORT STORY

STORY LENGTH

Before we jump in here, I want to make it clear that I'm generalizing on some of the definitions and requirements. It's important to understand that different markets (publishers) have different definitions of short story length. While one market might consider short story length to be 1000 to 5000 words, another might require a minimum of 2500 words with a cap of 10,000 words for a short story call. Always check the market's definition in their submission guidelines to ensure you're submitting to the right places. The word count requirements I've listed here are intended to give you a general idea of how a short story is defined in terms of length. Even more complicating is the fact that some magazines have a required page count, rather than a word count. That page count is frequently the magazine page count or how many pages it will take up in its final form in that publication. It is *not* your Microsoft Word count (or that of another text program) unless they specifically say so.

A short story should be between 1000 and 8000 words, with some markets going up to 10,000 for their short story requirements. Anything under 1000 words is considered flash fiction. Anything over the 8000 words is a novelette (8000 to 15,000), novella (15,000 to 40,000), or novel (over 40,000 words), depending upon the lengths. Again, specific markets will vary on what word count they accept and what their definitions of the various categories are. Always check the specific submission guidelines. This is going to be our mantra, so you can expect to see me repeating this over and over throughout the book. Why? Because people consistently ignore the submission guidelines when submitting, and it can mean the difference between your story being read in the first place and an automatic rejection.

THE BASICS

With the word count out of the way, we can jump into the dynamics of short stories. First, it's time for another disclaimer: much of this information is generalized. I don't believe in setting hard and fast rules on writing (submission requirements, yes, writing, no). What I'm passing along are tips to help you simplify your story into something that can stay short instead of growing up into a novel, novella, or novelette. Even then, a novella or novelette may be more closely related to a short story than a novel. It depends, which is a pain to hear. I realize that. But it will always depend upon the dynamics of your specific story and what you've done with it.

Edgar Allan Poe said, "A short story must have a single mood and every sentence must build towards it." In other words, the plot of a short story isn't going to be full of a billion different threads and subplots. That's a novel, and if you start out with a complicated storyline you're already past the point of writing a short story. With a short, you're trying to present a single, concentrated idea. Don't be fooled—a short story must still have a beginning, a middle, and an end. Writing short is not a license to throw the storyline or plot out the window. It must still be a complete story with a plot arc.

Some ways to boil your story down are to limit the number of characters to one or two main characters or points-of-view, limit the settings to less than three while making them vivid and immediate, limit the timeframe to one that's shorter and doesn't jump around, and limit your plotlines to one or possibly two. Even better is being able to focus in on one main character and a single, significant plotline that occurs in a brief span of time in one place. If you're completely new to short stories, this should be your goal. Simplifying a story down to its main ingredients and removing the fluff is going to help you learn how to write short. You can always expand on it later.

To be clear, when I refer to simplifying the story, I'm talking about removing the extras, the ornamentation, that aren't at all necessary to the story, but that we're used to putting into novel-length writing. This in no way implies that a short story can't be full of detail and beauty, only that every ingredient of the story must be vital to the plot and the character. Whimsical asides and unnecessary details will only hinder a short story.

Character, setting, and plot are just as vital in short stories as they are in novels. They are possibly even more important, because they must be used to immerse the reader in the story immediately. This doesn't necessarily mean starting in the middle of physical action, which people often default to when they try to address creating an immediate hook. It means that the writer must find a creative way to introduce the reader to the main character quickly and give the reader a reason to keep reading. It might seem like a reader would give a short story an equivalent amount of time to get engaged as they would require from a novel, but this isn't true. When someone sits down to read a short story, they expect to finish that story in one sitting, possibly with the idea of reading several short stories in a row. Which means they'll put the story down faster if they don't read something right away that makes them want to proceed.

The reader needs to be intrigued as soon as they start reading. This can be done by creating such an interesting character that they want to know more about them and what they're about to face. This requires skipping the useless appearance descriptions and diving into the meat of the character, their skeletal structure. What makes them tick? Are they facing a moral dilemma, a crush, or a dangerous situation? Perhaps the story starts with the character caught up in trying to make a difficult decision. Maybe they're fleeing something. It could also be that they're funny and charming, and the reader wants to get to know them.

I'm speaking in the singular here, because that's the best way to start out your short story writing. If you plan on having more than one important character (hopefully no more than two in this case or three if you're stretching), you'll have to introduce the other characters in rapid succession. If they pop up in the middle of the story, there had better be a good reason for doing so, and they must be introduced so the reader has an instant feel for them. A good way to introduce any character is through dialogue and actions. Presenting their current view through thoughts, observations, and reactions, whether thought or spoken, can be effective, as well. What this is doing is showing the reader who they're dealing with and what that character is facing, rather than telling the reader. It's an organic way to set the characterization right from the start, and hopefully draw the reader into their world.

The scene must also be set quickly. This can be done through the senses of the character and brief description. Don't spend even a single paragraph on scene description. The introduction of the character, the setting, and even the conflict, at least in part, can be addressed right away through what is occurring in the now.

Example: *Reggie ran through the woods, the foliage as thick as the scent of pine. Branches slapped him in the face and tore at his skin. He risked shooting a look over his shoulder to gauge how far behind they were and nearly tripped over a hidden stump. His breaths ripped through his throat and chest, his heart beating fast and hard, a frightened creature trying to escape his ribcage.*

The reader now knows several things: the character is in a deep pine forest, they're running from something or someone, and they're frightened. The opening doesn't have to feature someone running for their lives, though.

Example: *Sandy rearranged her papers in their file for the fifth time. She shot a look at the other end of the conference table, where Maria sat, an oasis of calm and confidence in her neatly pressed power suit. The other woman's gaze drifted in her direction and Sandy jerked and looked down at the folder again, her chair squeaking loudly for perhaps the hundredth time in the last five minutes. The scent of coffee filled the room, as rich as Maria's voice. Unable to help it, Sandy's gaze slid up the table to Maria once more, taking in the folder that sat before her, in which Sandy's fate hid.*

What do we know about this character? She's waiting for something, she's nervous or excited, it's job related, and the source of this angst is the woman in the suit. If, with this second example, the writer were to interject a thought, even more could be known about the character and the situation. All of this could be done in a few lines or a single paragraph. Both involve conflict, but only one of these is about a physically dangerous situation. Yet the reader has been dropped directly into the "action." Notice that there's still some description. Using the senses to pull the reader in can help get to the meat more quickly, as well. It's setting the scene in a few words. Brevity doesn't mean dropping all description. If that description is helping to introduce a character, setting, or situation, it should be included, but kept brief and wrapped in with the rest of the text. Emotions and using the senses can pull the reader in more quickly and thoroughly, because you're appealing to known quantities. For example, a reader will understand fright if they've ever been afraid. And the scent of an orange will be known to most. The thing about senses is that using them in a story can trigger a sense memory in the reader, causing an immediate reaction. That, paired with overall familiarity, can be powerful.

Addressing the conflict early on is another way to set up the story quickly and intrigue the reader right away. The above examples have done this, but there are countless other ways to do so. Making the conflict apparent also helps to set the tone and plot of the rest of the story, showing the reader what kind of ride they're in for. To repeat myself once again, this doesn't mean there has to be immediate physical action. What I mean by physical action is someone running or fighting or doing something physical that's meant to get the reader's heart pumping and flat out stick them in the middle of a fight or scary incident. Trying to do this often leads to an empty or useless scene that conveys little about the ultimate conflict or the character.

There are all kinds of ways to get the reader's heart pumping, whether through fear, excitement, or lust. It depends upon what kind of story they've signed on to read, but it should involve some kind of suspense. Starting the story in the middle of the action entails starting partway into a situation, interaction, or event, rather than trying to come at it from the beginning. What's more interesting, joining a character on their drive to work, where nothing happens, or sticking them in the boardroom where tension is building, because they're already at work and waiting for a specific incident to occur that could be seconds or minutes away? Expectation builds tension, and tension creates a hook.

In a short story, a slow build up is going to be less effective than it might be in a longer piece. There's less room to pull all the threads in with slow reveals. The pace must be quicker in a short story, and a slow burn is going to have a different definition. The writer only has a matter of pages in which to tell their story, rather than chapters. Sometimes this will entail starting closer to the climax, rather than utilizing the twisty-turns that go all over the place before getting to the point that novels often engage. If a portion of the *The Hobbit* were to be extracted as a short story, it would start somewhere vital and address one thread of the story. Whether that might be starting with Bilbo looking up at the mountain in which Smaug rests or the moment he finds the entrance to Smaug's cave, the important takeaway here is to start the story in the right place. Certainly, if the short story were to be about his interaction with Smaug or his battle of wits with Golem, the story would not start with Gandalf inviting him on the journey and it would not end at the same place the book does, but rather after the interaction with Smaug or Golem. It would start at the beginning of the correct scene and would have that single plotline in mind, not the entirety of the book. In other words, there's no way *The Hobbit* could be made into a short story in its entirety. The storyline doesn't allow for that.

Further to this, the pace is important, vital even. Paragraphs that are too long may turn the reader off. Varying sentence structure and length can help move the story along. A short story should keep the reader moving forward without giving them breaks, such as a novel might with a calm chapter or with the location of a chapter break that allows the reader to take a breath. While there can be lulls, they shouldn't be so sedate as to stop the forward progression of the story.

They should be natural and still contribute some aspect of the storyline or characterization.

In any length of writing, making sentences shorter and choppier can help increase the speed of reading, which picks up the pace. This can be especially helpful in an action sequence or a frightening or suspenseful section. At the same time, longer sentences can slow the reader down and make them linger more over an important section. Vary the rhythms and patterns in your writing in order to keep the reader from getting bored and to give them a taste of the sensations they should be feeling as they read.

This is as good a place as any to address backstory. Backstory is frowned upon in novel-writing, as well, but in short stories it absolutely must have a purpose that directly contributes to the story or it shouldn't exist. Instead of laying it all out, give the reader a portion or simply hint at it. Create tension between two characters by hinting that they've had a bad experience in the past or a sordid history exists between them, but let the reader wonder what that incident might be and how far the main character might be willing to take their dislike or defensiveness against the other character. The film *A Promising Young Woman* does this well. The main character is obviously bent on righting certain wrongs throughout the film. It is, in fact, her driving purpose. However, the moviegoer doesn't find out what happened, in general, until about seventy-five percent of the way into the film, and even then, it's not all laid out for the audience. There are implications that the audience can apply their own personal experiences or assumptions to, and it's all devastating in its own right.

When hinting at backstory, it's important to get the tone of the story right so the reader knows which direction in which to send their own assumptions. That tone is set through everything I've already mentioned: character, setting, plot, conflict. Taking the boardroom example, the tone could vary between the character being afraid they're about to be fired or being excited because they think they're about to get a promotion. How that initial scene is fleshed out will allow the reader to feel the expected emotions while they wait through the suspense with the main character. The character can be thinking about how they'll pay their bills if the worst happens or they could be thinking about how they'll spend the extra cash that comes with the promotion.

In terms of arcs within the story, a short story does need to have a full plot arc and a character arc. A full transformation arc isn't necessarily going to come into play as much as it would in a novel. The character must be impacted, but they don't have to face as *much* change as they might in a novel. The aim with a short story is to incite a reaction, whether that be calm, fear, lust, intrigue, anger, or some other emotion, and to tell a complete and satisfying story. If the character changes drastically during that story, all the better. If they do not, the reader must at least know how the character has been impacted and what *has* changed. This is an extension of making sure the reader cares what happens to the character, which is how they'll be pulled into the story, as well as how tension or suspense can be created.

If you do not give your story the full plot arc, you've likely written a vignette, which is purely a moment in time presented for the reader's pleasure or an immediate reaction, not a short story. In short stories, the resolution needs to be impactful. It can bring the reader relief, make them think on the subject after they've put the book down, or incite further emotion. Looking back at *The Hobbit*, any short story from it would have to end with Bilbo either failing or succeeding in his mission. In the case of him facing off with Golem, were that to be a short story, it would end when he safely got out of the cave with the ring as both his prize and his means of escape. The totality of the story would have been his getting lost from a larger group of travelers (the beginning), his interactions with Golem and finding of the ring (middle), and his escape with the ring (conclusion). No other plots or major characters would exist, and the conclusion would be a satisfying one and, in this case, a happy one, with him off to find his party, now in possession of a prize and safely away from the threat he had faced.

Twist endings are far more common in short stories than in longer works, and can often change the entire meaning of the story that came beforehand, at least if they're skillfully handled. A twist may have the intention of making the reader think back through everything that's already happened and view it through a different pair of eyes or with a changed mindset. Note, however, that a plot twist must be supported by the story that came before, meaning it can't just be a cheap trick that negates everything that already happened. Instead, it is meant to reveal what already happened in a different light.

Much of writing a short story is the same as writing a novel, only more compact. This extends to the characters, the setting, the plot, the storyline, and the pace. Timelines are different for short stories, but the overall arc is the same. Either way, you should be writing a story that grabs the reader's interest and won't let them go. They should be entertained and made to feel something about the story, and they should come away from their reading experience with the same sort of satisfaction a novel would offer, meaning a well-told story with a beginning, middle, and end, and a resolution that leaves them satisfied that the plot has been tied up, even if that doesn't mean a happy ending. There are genres that do require a happy ending, such as romance, which requires either happily ever after or happily ever after for now. In a mystery or suspense, the mystery must be solved and the culprit caught. There's more freedom in horror, where there's not necessarily an expectation of a happy ending. Still, an ending must exist.

A-B-C-D-E METHOD

Wrapping this all back together is the A-B-C-D-E method, which I've found attributed to other authors, but first read about in Anne Lamott's *Bird by Bird: Some Instructions on Writing and Life,* where she attributed it to Alice Adams. To summarize the concept, a short story must contain **A**ction (the thing that draws the reader in and makes them want to know the rest of the story), **B**ackground (what's happening and how the character came to be here, plus why the reader should care), **C**onflict (what the character needs, what they're trying to achieve, and what is standing in the way of it—can be internal or external, but is usually both), **D**evelopment (the plot/story arc and the actions undertaken by the character to address the conflict(s)), and **E**nding (what is the final resolution to the conflict?). This is a simplified way to set up your story, and it wraps up the bulk of what we've discussed.

CONCLUSION

One way to get the pacing of short stories down is to ensure you read short stories. It's the closest to osmosis any of us can get. Look for magazines and anthologies in the genre in which you write; buy "best of" collections, like the annual The Best Horror of the Year, edited by Ellen Datlow, long-term collections such as The World's Greatest Short Stories, edited by James Daley, or diaspora-specific collections, such as The Best Short Stories by Black Writers, 1899-1967: The Classic Anthology, edited by Langston Hughes; and check out collections by authors you already enjoy reading. Many novel authors have had at least one short story published. There are also hundreds of short stories available online. A simple search can bring up a variety to read. Narrow it down by searching based on specific authors or genres. Two websites offering short stories free to read are www.classicshorts.com and www.americanliterature.com/twenty-great-american-short-stories.-com. Pay attention as you're reading short stories and notice what they do with the pacing, the characters, the set-up, the plot, and more. It can be eye opening and make the flow of short story writing come more naturally.

Another option is to take what you consider to be a well-written short story and retype it in order to manually feel that flow. It's a good idea to start by simply retyping the story exactly the same as it was originally published so you can get the feel of it. The exercise can then be expanded by retyping the story but changing the verbs and nouns in order to make it a new story. To be very clear, if you do this second portion of the exercise, this is not a story that would be publishable. That would still be plagiarism. The purpose of this is not to have a saleable story, but to hone your craft and get a better understanding of the dynamics of short story writing.

In all, it may take some time to get the patterns and rhythms of short story writing down, but that's what editing is for. With practice, it will become more natural. Don't panic if they run long at first, or if you're struggling to fit the story into the space allotted. Just keep trying. It will be worth it in the end.

CHAPTER SUMMARY

- Short stories are typically considered to be between 1000 and 8000 words, but different markets will have their own definitions.
- Short stories must have a beginning, a middle, and an end.
- There should be no more than 1-2 major characters.
- There should be no more than a single plotline, with the possibility of a secondary, minor plotline.
- Limit settings and timeframes.
- Start the story in the correct place and end it in a satisfying way.
- Character, setting, conflict, and plot are vital to short stories, and must be established immediately.
- Dialogue, thoughts, observations, and reactions can help set character, plot, and setting.
- Tension is vital.
- The pace must be quicker in a short story, with slow builds and backstory reduced or removed entirely.
- Twist endings can be powerful in a short story.
- Vary sentence length and paragraphing.
- There must be a full plot arc, but character arc can be limited as long as the character is impacted.
- Read short stories in order to be able to write short stories.

CHAPTER 2
EDITING

We're going to touch briefly on editing. In general, if you know how to edit any piece of writing, you know how to edit a short story. However, there are some short story-specific things to keep in mind when editing.

The first thing to do is set that fresh story aside for a period of time. This completely depends upon what works for you, but it can be anywhere from a couple days to a couple weeks. Or longer. The thing about a short story is that it will often be finished in a brief enough time that the details will be too fresh in your mind as you re-read it. This will make it so mistakes get missed, because your brain will automatically fill in the errors with what it knows should be there.

It's also a good idea to read the story aloud at some point during editing. Really, editing of anything can be better if it's heard aloud. Another option is using a program that reads your piece aloud for you. There are several available, including some free ones, but the quality and the voice vary. Do a search on text-to-speech software and look through the options if this is something that interests you. At the time of this book being written, some of the best reviewed free pieces of software are Balabolka, Natural Reader, and WordTalk. Microsoft has their own version entitled ReadAloud. And some of the best rated paid versions are Amazon Polly, Linguatec, Capti, and NaturalReader. Note that some of the paid versions do have free tiers, but those didn't make the lists of best free software. Hearing a story read aloud is different than reading it on the page, and there are different types of errors that will be caught this way, including issues with voice, pacing, and sentence fluency. Even word choice might stand out. If you stumble over a word, your reader likely will, too. Look for the flow of the story and anywhere that catches you up. The reader is less likely to continue reading with each example of a stumbling block. If it pulls them out of the story, it's a lot easier to put the story down. That's the last thing any writer wants.

WORD COUNT/LENGTH

A big thing to check for is word count. This is going to matter more if there's a specific market you wish to submit the story to. Editors don't take kindly to someone ignoring their word count require- ments, and it can be an automatic rejection if they open the document and see that it's outside their requested count. In fact, I attended a panel at Worldcon consisting of magazine editors and they all said that an easy thing for them to check was word count right at the beginning. If it was outside the parameters of the submission guide- lines, they wouldn't read any further. Don't try to squeak through with even a few words over the maximum or under the minimum. Maybe a big name can do that, but the rest of us need to stick to the requirements.

I can count on one hand the number of times I've modified a story's word count in order to be able to submit it to a specific market. I prefer to keep my story as it is, rather than to chase the word count for a specific market. That comes down to personal choice. Once you've written short stories for a while, you can usually go in with a specific word count in mind and hit pretty close to it. Again, that's about rhythm and paying attention to the word count throughout the writing process. If you're almost to the word count and haven't hit the middle of your story, it's obvious that the story won't be within word count and modification is needed right away. That's better than discovering it after the fact, when you have a lovely, shiny story that you don't want to brutalize.

If the story is just slightly over or under word count, it's easy to add or delete a few words. It's when the difference is significant that it becomes a major issue. If you've considered whether you want to plow forward and change the word count to get into this particular market, it's time to look at the story dynamics and see either what's missing or what's unnecessary. The beauty of short stories is how much can be conveyed in such a small word count.

Remove:

- Unnecessary characters
- Scenes that don't contribute anything significant to the story
- Backstory
- Extraneous arcs that don't impact the overall arc of the story
- Overzealous descriptions
- Other things of that nature.

In other words, what you're looking to do, if needing to cut words, is keep the meat of the story and remove the garnish.

On the flipside of that, if the need is to increase the word count, don't try to add in wasted words and empty pieces. Either the story can be expanded or it can't.

Look for:

- Unexplored character traits and history
- Uncompleted arcs
- A way to flesh out the middle of the story
- A secondary character that can be buffed up
- Other content-rich and content-applicable changes

Anything added should still contribute to the story. Otherwise, as much as you may want to get into that market, they're going to notice that the story is full of fluff, which will lead to a rejection. If the story was written toward a specific call and cannot be made to work and still maintain its strengths, it might be more worth it to write a completely different story or pass by this particular call. There will be other markets to submit it to that will appreciate it at the length it was meant to be.

CRITIQUE GROUPS & BETA READERS

A great way to find out if a story works is to either join a critique group —a group of people that exchange stories and give each other feedback —or ask specific people to be beta readers—a first reader who reads the entire thing and gives feedback. Reciprocity is built into a critique group, but with a beta reader you're asking an individual to do you a favor. Consider what you can do in return for that favor, such as offering to do the same for them in the future or, for non-writers, buying them dinner or a drink. It is important that stories be edited thoroughly before turning them into any sort of critique group or to a beta reader, or else they'll have to spend all their time line editing instead of looking at the story as a whole.

For a critique group, be careful which group you choose. Whether putting one together or joining one that already exists, it's important that the members all be people whose opinions you respect, whose writing you can enjoy, and who are all equally dedicated to the group. There are many pitfalls to critique groups, but the ones that work can improve your writing significantly and teach you how to watch for your most common errors. At the same time, critiquing others' work can often be eye-opening to mistakes you make. It can bring about epiphanies concerning things you do that you hadn't noticed before, because it can be easier to spot in someone else's work.

Writing about critique groups could take up an entire book, due to the many varied groups I've been part of, but for the purposes of this book, I just want to address the basics. When joining or creating a critique group, ensure there are rules in place.

These rules can include things such as:

- How often the group meets (weekly, bi-monthly, or monthly)
- Whether group members can respond or argue when they're being critiqued (some of the best groups I've been part of

required that the person being critiqued listen quietly and take notes unless asked a direct question)
- Genres allowed to be submitted
- How feedback should be given
- Word limits for how much can be turned in at once (as in, don't turn in a novel or six full chapters at a single meeting)
- Attendance requirements (miss three meetings in a row and you're out)
- The level of writer allowed in (whether beginners can take part or if everyone needs to be at about the same level)
- Other concerns of that nature that may come back to bite members in the behind

With any group of people, setting up a group where you have specific expectations requires voicing those expectations from the beginning. Otherwise, there will be frustrations and hurt feelings. It's also a good idea to build in a review process in case there's a problematic member. One member not performing or showing up can ruin the entire group for everyone. It's frustrating to critique everyone else's work and have only two people give a critique in return or to have someone who never turns anything in, but critiques everyone else. Either way, that person isn't fully contributing to the group, and they may need to be removed.

The benefits of having a regular critique group are:

- Increased productivity
- Improvement in writing quality
- Feedback that can help polish a story
- A writing family or kinship with other writers you can depend on

People are more likely to get their words in and be productive when they have someone expecting them to have work ready to turn in regularly. That productivity leads to more pieces available to be submitted for publication, which is typically the end goal.

Drawbacks of critique groups are:

- Dealing with possible toxicity
- Frustration over people not doing their part
- Getting nasty feedback instead of constructive feedback (there always seems to be someone who thinks they should be the Simon Cowell)
- Loss of motivation.

If the group consists of people who don't understand how to give constructive feedback or they don't understand how to write the genre you're submitting, they can do a significant amount of damage to your ego and, thus, your work and conviction. I used to think it was best to have a mixed group, because I found beginners sometimes gave better feedback on overall story and plot, while the more advanced folks hit deeper notes. However, too many times the beginners give up because the more advanced writers expect too much out of them. I've found myself in groups where I was pulling my punches and trying to focus on one thing that a beginner could work on, rather than giving them full feedback, because I didn't want them to get hurt and give up, but this made my work of critiquing them much harder than it otherwise would have been. Nobody wants to get or give a manuscript full of red marks, if they can help it. Having said that, it's absolutely vital to give honest feedback. Otherwise, the entire exercise is a waste of time for both parties.

As far as beta readers, they are often a better option for novels than short stories, but it doesn't hurt to have a single person read your story if you have concerns. With beta readers, it's best to provide a list of specific questions and leave a space for any additional notes. What is it, specifically, that you want them to address in the piece? Whereas critique groups are going to go over the more surface issues since they're reading multiple manuscripts for each meeting, a beta reader should be going deeper, and it helps them to know what you are questioning so they can pay attention to that. In addition, it's best to set a deadline for when they need to have their feedback turned in. The person chosen as a beta reader should once again be someone you trust to do the work and give quality feedback on a timeline, but they still need a deadline. Most people work better with one. This is especially important if the story is due for a specific publication with a deadline of their own. You need to ensure that you have time to go over the feedback and incorporate any you wish to keep into the manuscript before turning it in.

On this note, a mistake beginners make with being critiqued is to think that everything everyone says is correct, and that everything must be incorporated into the manuscript. This is far from true. Each person will see each story in a different way. If what they say rings true, then you should incorporate their changes. If it doesn't, examine whether it makes sense and discard it if it doesn't. There is no rule that you have to accept someone else's opinion of your story. Some things to consider if you're unsure are that person's overall writing experience, your personal dynamic, and their familiarity with your genre and the form. For example, I was usually the only one turning in short stories and/or horror in each group, and some of my critique partners never read either—from them, I expected very specific types of feedback that might be helpful, and I was prepared to dismiss the rest. In the end, the story is yours. It needs to be what you want it to be and what you're comfortable with. Take all feedback with a grain of salt and consider whether it has value to you. That also means questioning any knee jerk reactions you might have to feedback they give. Are you resisting the feedback because it's not actually applicable or because the truth hit a little too close to home?

FINAL THOUGHTS ON EDITING

For my final edit, which means the one that follows any basic line editing and critiquing, I like to print up the story and edit it on paper. Just as with hearing a story aloud, seeing it on paper can reveal missed mistakes. This should be the final polish. This is where you might catch formatting mistakes, as well, which might be easier to miss on a screen. At this point, you should be intimately familiar with this story and looking for the little things, because the story issues should have already been resolved in previous edits, which for me, would have been done before I let others set eyes on it for critique or beta reading. I tend to commingle the final polish with incorporating any final critiques, which allows me to have those critiques on paper alongside a polished version of my story. It's easier to accept or decline the feedback that way, but that's just how it works for me.

This chapter has erred toward holding all editing until the story has been completed. Some people prefer to edit as they write. This is true for any length of writing. Personally, I feel it interrupts the flow of my creativity and slows down the writing, which is why my process involves writing the story first, whether I'm writing short form or long form. That may not be an issue for you, so if it bothers you to hold your edits or you simply feel you'd prefer to edit as you go, give it a try. If it doesn't feel right, you can always attempt it my way and save the editing. For those who tend to get thrown from a story or suffer writer's block, that can sometimes be attributed to not turning off the inner editor while writing. Not everyone will be impacted the same way. The only way to figure out how you edit best is to try each method and feel out where you're most comfortable. It may also morph at some point, and you may need to change up your game. That can happen with any stage of writing. Being resistant to change might stymie your creativity, so try different things when you're struggling. Ultimately, it may help you iron out the issues and get back to the important part: your creativity.

Your mileage may vary, and you may do things in a different order. That's perfectly okay. As I've mentioned before and will likely mention again, all of this comes down to what you discover works best for you. No two writers have the same process. Experiment as you go, and your processes should grow right alongside your writing.

To end this chapter, here are some questions to consider when wrapping up your editing:

- Have you written a full story with a well-developed plot?
- Have you opened in a way that draws the reader in right away?
- Does your middle keep the reader engaged?
- Have you established a character the reader cares about or is curious about?

- Have you created a story arc that includes a beginning, a middle, and an end?
- Have you created a satisfying conclusion?
- Did you leave time after writing to make the story less familiar before editing?
- Are you happy with your results?

CHAPTER SUMMARY

- You can either edit as you write or save it until the end.
- Editing as you write may cause creative slumps.
- It helps to set a story aside for a period of time before attempting to do a full edit.
- Reading aloud may help catch nuances not caught while reading silently.
- Printing a story up and editing on paper may help cause errors missed on the screen.
- Don't submit a story to a market if your word count is outside their requirements.
- If you wish to change your word count to be able to submit it to a specific publication/market, make sure cuts don't hurt the story and that additions truly add to the story and aren't just filling.
- Consider joining a critique group to get feedback on your stories before submitting them to markets.
- Consider getting the help of an individual beta reader (or several).
- Not all feedback will be accurate for the story you've created. Listen, consider, and decide whether it sounds right or applicable. Do NOT take all feedback as correct and apply it to your story before carefully considering it.
- In the end, the story is yours. You make the final decision on what feedback to apply.

CHAPTER 3
WRITING EXERCISES

WRITING EXERCISES

- Take a short story written by someone else and figure out the A-B-C-D-E of it. Break it down into the Action, Background, Conflict, Development, and Ending. If you're looking for an extra challenge, take just those elements of the story and write a new one based off them.
- Write two different introductory paragraphs: one with physical conflict and one with mental/emotional conflict. If you want to go further, write the full stories.
- Write a short story of any theme that includes the following words: violin, elm, statue, cat, camera, and clown.
- Take any movie and choose one aspect of it to write a short story about. The story must have a beginning, middle, and end, a plot, and a full story arc.
- Write a short story on any theme, but be sure to include at least one example of each of the senses. Don't just say: "She smelled an orange." Say: "The crisp, sharp tang of the orange filled the air."
- If you've ever received a rewrite request or a critique that

you didn't agree with, attempt to rewrite your story using that feedback to see what happens. Does it change the entire story? Does it improve it or make it weaker?

- To see what type of editing works best for you, set a timer for a preset time (say, 15 minutes) and write without editing at all. Once done, set another timer for the same amount of time and edit while writing. Which way do you get the most done? How bothersome is it not to edit? Consider how it felt mentally. Did editing interrupt the flow of the story or were you able to continue more comfortably with the edits done?

PART THREE
WHAT'S NEXT? PRE-SUBMISSIONS OVERVIEW

What to Expect:

- Market research
- Submission resources
- Writing contests
- Submission guidelines
- Contracts
- Pay
- Reprints
- Simultaneous submissions
- Multiple submissions
- Formatting
- Writing a bio

CHAPTER 4
MARKET RESEARCH

B efore you can submit, you need to do market research in order to find out where you can possibly submit a story. "Market," in this case, means a publication, such as a magazine or an anthology. There are countless resources available for this, but it helps to have some information about your piece and the market first.

GENRE

Firstly, you need to know what genre you're trying to submit. If you're not sure of your genre, some simple research online should help. As will reading publications of one genre or another.

Here are some basic definitions to get you started:

- Speculative Fiction: Writing about things that are fantastical or that change the world or people into something different. A genre used to look at our world through a different lens. Examples include fantasy, which tends to be about writing fantastical and mythological-type creatures or to occur in different worlds; science fiction, which modifies the world in a scientific or technological sense and may take place in space or on other planets; and horror, which is oddly wedged into speculative fiction, and involves creating horror or terror for the reader, whether psychological, gory, or otherwise horrifying.

- Mystery/Thriller/Suspense: Each typically involves a crime or has a mystery to solve, from the softer, such as finding a missing item, to the heavier, such as finding a murderer. Mystery tends to leave the reader out of the loop, while a thriller or suspense might put the reader in the perpetrator's point-of-view. Thrillers and suspense tend to stress an ongoing danger and raise the stakes. Suspense may start out slower than a thriller and build the suspense more as the story continues.

- Romance/Women's Fiction: A romance is about the emotional interaction between characters. It can be paired with other genres, such as a thriller or a fantasy, but romance must be a vital part of the story. Women's fiction often involves romance, but focuses on women's issues and/or the relationships between women.

- Literary: The stress here is put on the style of the writing. The story can cover a lot of different ground, but the writing itself is a focus and the story is typically character-driven more than driven by plot. It can come across as poetic. Beautifully written, but hard to define stories may be put in this category.

- Historical/Western: Historical stories are set in the past. They can be combined with other genres, such as romance or science fiction. They may involve action and adventure or be focused on issues and overcoming them. Westerns are specific to the time of the Wild West or westward expansion.

- Memoir/True Crime/Nonfiction: Memoir involves true stories that occurred in an individual's life. Nonfiction is about something real, something that actually occurred. Creative nonfiction is the same, but leaves wiggle room for expanding on the story by filling in the blanks. True crime involves real life crimes.

- New Adult/Young Adult/Middle Grade/Children's: While these can be paired with any other genre, they must be aimed at the correct age group. New adult stories tend to deal with issues that people in their twenties hit as they try to come into their own, such as leaving family behind, engaging in careers, and setting off on their own. Young adult is aimed at teens and the issues they face. Both NA and YA can deal with very serious topics and have more license than MG and children's to explore them. Middle grade is aimed at pre-teens, while children's is aimed at more elementary school level children. Whichever category the story falls into, it's generally expected that most of the characters, especially the main character, will fit into the age group at which the story is aimed. So the main character in a YA should be a teenager and the main story in a children's book should be younger than a pre-teen.

A lot of markets narrow it down to a major genre, which can include smaller aspects of that genre, or sub-genres. For example, a speculative fiction market might ask for only sword and sorcery fantasy or space-based science fiction. A romance publication may ask for only paranormal romance. Literary magazines will often accept submissions of different genres as long as the writing is literary, but they'll also often take memoir and similar types of narrative. It should be clear from their website what they're publishing. This is even more true for those that narrow it down more completely, such as magazines or anthologies that are only looking for supernatural horror, thrillers involving serial killers, or male/male romance. They will often stress what they're seeking specifically in their guidelines.

When you're trying to narrow down what genre you're writing, it can help to go beyond searching for definitions online by reading anthologies and magazines and seeing what genre they are. There are many magazines available for free online. Amazon is also good resource for this. It's easy to plug a genre in and see what kinds of books come up. Click on some of these and read the blurbs. Read samples if they have the "See Inside" option. The library is also a great place to go to do this research, because certain genres are split out. The same is true for a brick-and-mortar bookstore. Take some time to look through books in the genre you think you're writing and ensure you've got it down. When it comes to the tighter sub-genres, that can also be plugged in to a search bar or on Amazon to further narrow down your search. This should at least give you a feel for it. If all else fails, ask a friend to read your story and tell you what genre they believe you've written. It's most helpful if this person is a writer, but staunch readers can also help narrow it down. There are times where you'll just have to do your best and pick the genre. The worst that can happen is your story getting rejected.

RESOURCES

In terms of resources geared specifically to helping writers figure out where to submit, there are websites like Duotrope and Submission Grinder that provide a form where anybody can plug in information and have the publications available narrowed down. Note that Duotrope is a for-fee service and Submission Grinder is free. These websites also allow those submitting to record when and where they've submitted, and will track how long those pieces have been out and even when to send a query or follow-up.

The way these two sites work is to put up a form with various categories that the writer fills out using drop-down menus. For example, the form will have a space for the genre, subgenres, story length, rate of pay the writer is seeking, and submission type (electronic, by mail, etc.). There are further categories intended to allow the writer to whittle it down to the most specific market available, if desired. The writer selects the pertinent information then hits the search button. The sites then bring up listings of the markets that match the details provided, and the writer can click through to the market websites to glean further information and determine if their story will be a fit. We'll discuss fit more shortly, but in the meantime I'm talking about whether the story is appropriate for the chosen publication. There are several items to check off in order to arrive at this conclusion, which you'll find in Chapters Four and Five.

Screen grab of the Duotrope publisher search page

These websites don't necessarily have all the submission specifications, because they depend upon the publishers to provide that information to the website and to have it on their own web pages for writers to find. Not all publishers know about these sites or choose to use them. As such, it's prudent to have other resources to find publishers. No worries! There are plenty. A good place to find publishers is via the magazines and anthologies you already enjoy reading. Go to their websites and figure out how to submit. If it's an anthology, chances are that the publisher will put out future anthologies, so it's a good idea to subscribe to a newsletter if they offer one or just remember to check back occasionally for possible publications.

These publications also often have social media (everyone should, these days). Like and follow the social media form you prefer that they offer. Make sure to compare their social media to ensure they don't prefer to stick with a different type, such as a publisher who, despite having both Twitter and Facebook, only randomly tweets, but steadily posts updates on their Facebook page. In addition to social media for specific publications, there a lot of Facebook groups that exist to pass around news of submission calls. They cover a lot of categories, so searches can turn up general submission call pages or ones that announce calls for submissions in a particular genre or for specific pay. For instance, there are "for the love" pages (meaning no pay) and pro pay pages that will only post about calls in those categories. I typically follow specific genre submission call pages, so I can choose whether a call sounds interesting enough, despite not paying, that I might want to submit anyway. Some of the best projects are those that don't pay professional rates, but have a fun idea for a theme.

There are also blogs and websites that will post about markets seeking story submissions. For example, there's the *Published to Death* blog, which lists submission calls for all genres. *Horror Tree* posts horror markets seeking submissions. *Ralan* posts about speculative fiction calls. Do a search based on the genre you're writing to see if anyone is putting out calls for submissions.

It's not only about online, either. If you're reading collections of reprints (stories already printed elsewhere), such as "Best of" titles, they must have a section where they list where the stories were originally published. Checking that page out, especially if you really liked a story or it felt like exactly the feel you're aiming to get published, can lead you to publications you might not have found elsewhere. Find where the story was previously published and look them up online. Sadly, magazines go out of print and publishers go under all the time, so a publication that existed when the story first came out may not anymore. Still, it's a chance worth taking.

If you know other authors publishing short stories, pay attention to where they're getting published. This can lead you to magazines and anthology publishers you might not have otherwise found. Note that anthologies are most often published by small publishers that use it as a way to get both their authors and their brand out in front of new readers. Those readers may read an anthology because their favorite author (or a friend or family member) is in it, find a new author they enjoyed, and seek out that author in other publications.

Finally, there's also an annual book that comes out called *Writer's Market*. Their 100th edition was released in 2021. While the book can be a bit pricey for those who don't have the extra money to spend, libraries usually carry a copy. The book provides a wide span of opportunities, including magazines, book publishers, literary agents, contests, and more, and can be a fantastic resource. Even stumbling across a slightly older version can provide plenty of publishing opportunities, though portions of the book will be outdated. For beginners with more than one item up for submission, it can be an acceptable cost. In fact, it's cheaper than a year of Duotrope, though you can't use it to keep track of your submissions the way you can Duotrope. It all boils down to what you're willing to spend on publishing resources and which type of resource will be the most helpful to you. Overwhelmingly, writers are trending toward the online resources, rather than the physical book. This may now increase, because *Writer's Market* was sold to Penguin Random House in 2019 and stopped providing an online resource at that time, though they'd previously had one available to those who purchased the book. Currently, their website simply provides links to where the book versions can be purchased.

There are many resources, with more popping up each day. Search online and try out different versions until you find what works best for you. That might be a printed book, like *Writer's Market*, or it could be one of the countless online places that source the information, such as blogs, websites, submission platforms like Duotrope, or Facebook groups. It's probably not worth it to use every available resource, but you can narrow it down to the most helpful for you.

CHAPTER SUMMARY

- Figuring out your genre is an important first step in choosing the right market for your story.
- Major genres are Speculative Fiction, Mystery/Thriller, Romance/Women's Fiction, Historical/Western, Literary, Memoir/True Crime/Nonfiction, and NA/YA/MG/Children's.
- Websites like Duotrope and Submission Grinder can provide a way to search for open markets.
- Open markets can also be found on blogs, websites, Facebook groups, and other social media.
- Writer's Market is a print book resource for finding open markets, and can be found at a library sometimes if you don't wish to buy it.
- Look up where authors who write the same types of stories you do are getting published in order to find other open markets.

CHAPTER 5
SUBMISSION GUIDELINES

W hat's that thing I said I'd harp on? Oh yes, submission guidelines. This is the most important thing to check before sending a story out to any publisher. They will all have some sort of guidelines set, even if they're brief. Pay attention to what they say, because it can make or break a submission.

GENRE/THEME

In terms of what you'll find in submission guidelines, and what you should be looking for, there's a tidy list of details. Number one is the genre. Always make sure your story fits into the genre of the publication to which you're submitting. This can be tricky, especially when a story crosses multiple genres. In this instance, try to figure out which takes precedence. For example, there's romantic suspense, paranormal romance, urban fantasy, straight-up romance, and romance with a hint of mystery. Determining which aspect of the story is most important to it will help determine what genre to submit it under. Listing five genres as representing your story won't do you any favors with editors, and they'll likely move on to something else. It marks you as either unknowledgeable or unprofessional. Does the point of the story really revolve around the romance? If so, that's going to be the most important aspect, whether there's a mysterious killer or an elf involved. On the other hand, if the romance takes a back seat to the paranormal elements, you may have more of an urban fantasy or contemporary fantasy. You can only do your best to figure this out and see if an editor agrees with your decision.

A publication may have specific themes in addition to genre. For example, there might be a Christmas theme for any genre of magazine. A romance magazine might want only meet cutes. A mystery magazine may be on the lookout for heist stories. In the case of a themed issue or anthology, they'll list the theme and usually give some background information on it to help writers understand what it is they're looking for. Make sure you've matched both the theme and the genre. I'm not saying you can't stretch the theme out a tiny bit as long as it still appears to be a good match. I've submitted some stories that really stretched the theme, and landed invitations for future publications as a result, even though the stories didn't actually work for that particular call. They were close enough that I felt it was worth trying it out, but not quite right in the end. Don't send something entirely incompatible and think anything good will come of it. The editor isn't stupid and will know you're simply throwing any story at them. In fact, they'll know if you're intentionally stretching the theme, but if they can see why you did so, it might work out.

WORD COUNT

Second most important is the word count. Most publishers have a hard word count range they're after. Some will mention that a couple words over or under isn't a big deal, while others will say in their guidelines that they won't take even one word outside that range. Err on the side of the latter if it's not laid out. When figuring your word count, don't count any top of page matter, such as your name, the word count tally, the title, or your contact information. They want the word count of the actual story. If they're looking for short stories of 5000 to 10,000 words, they do not want your flash fiction piece of 200 words or your novella of 20,000 words. They want what they've asked for, and sending something outside of that range will get you auto-rejected.

READING PERIODS/DEADLINES

There may be specific reading periods, so that's something else to check for. While some magazines are always open for submissions, others have rolling cut-off dates or open sporadically when they've gotten through the previous bunch of submissions. Some may also have a different theme or different requirements for each submission window. They should clearly state this information in their submission guidelines. Don't push your luck or their patience by submitting during a closed window or after a deadline has passed. Those submissions will also go unread and get deleted without you being notified that it's happened.

OTHER GUIDELINES

Some editors put more guidelines and information on their submissions pages than others. Some will provide interested submitters with the very basics and nothing more, which is more common for editors wanting a wide variety of stories. Those who have more specific tastes will try to make those tastes clear to submitters in order to avoid frustration on both your parts. It's a pain to not know what an editor is looking for, but also to be that editor reading a bunch of things that don't interest them in the least. They're not writing these guidelines just to fill their time or waste yours. They're doing so because they've seen the same issues repeatedly and want to keep that from happening. Sometimes those frustrations leak over into the submission guidelines, and it's clear from the tone that they've reached the limit of their patience on the matter. Be sure to read through everything they've put within the guidelines and note them as compared to what you're submitting.

In those guidelines, some specificities might involve what type of story or what elements are allowed to be in it. Horror gives us some good examples. Horror publishers may say they don't like gore, perhaps, or that harm to children or animals is an automatic rejection. Some horror publishers might like a hint of comedy in their stories, while others might want only serious horror. There are all kinds of things that a publisher might specifically ask to include or exclude from stories, and it's best to note these. An example of a publisher who has specific lists of what they want and what they don't want is Neil Clarke of *Clarkesworld*, a speculative fiction magazine. He's been in the business a long time, and he updates the list when he finds another tired trope or a story he's getting too many of.

Other items of note in submission guidelines involve what must be included with the submission. For example, some will state what they want to see in the cover letter or the subject line of the email. They might have multiple anthology calls out or different magazines that get submissions to the same email. As such, they'll ask you to include the title of the magazine or anthology you're submitting to. Some want the author's name and story title in the subject line for ease of finding it among all the emails. Some want "submission" written in the subject line to be able to pick out a submission against all other communication happening in that email. We'll discuss later what to put in the subject line if there are no specifications, but as with everything else, always check to be sure there are no specifications instead of assuming there aren't.

For what they want in the cover letter, some will ask for a one- or two-sentence summary of the story, though they tend to be in the minority. Some want a full bio included, while others would prefer no personal information. Editors all process submissions in different ways, and they've set up their submission guidelines to hopefully streamline the process, which can include information requested in the cover letter and subject line. Things that make a busy editor's life busier or harder aren't going to be appreciated. Note what they ask for and be sure to include it, even if it goes against what you're accustomed to sending in a submission. This is true of all guidelines put out by an editor.

Other stipulations may involve the process of submitting and what to include. Each editor typically lists specific formats they'll accept the story in, such as .doc or .rtf. Many still don't accept .docx, though this window is narrowing. It all depends upon what software they're using on their end and how many readers they'll need to distribute the story to in order to get that acceptance or rejection. Not all stories are read by only one editor. In fact, for magazines there are frequently slush readers. These are folks who do the first read-through of stories submitted in order to determine if the editors would want to see the story or not. *Apex Magazine*, for example, uses slush readers. If the submitting writer gets through the slush reader to an editor they will get a notification that they're getting a second read. If not, the rejection is from the slush reader.

They will also specify how they want to receive it. Should the story be pasted into the body of the email, meaning no attachments, or should it be submitted via a submission portal (a website or software used for submissions, such as Submittable) or as an attachment? There are a handful of publications that only take mailed submissions. I avoid those due to my personal preferences, but that doesn't mean there's anything wrong with that type of submission. You may be just fine with submitting a story via postal mail. Be sure to check their preferences on this, such as whether a SASE (Self-Addressed Stamped Envelope) should be included; whether the pages should be stapled, paper-clipped, or loose; and whatever else they might request. Beyond those publications, though, most want it emailed or done via a submission portal. Some have their own portals, while others go through paid services. It's a good idea to have a Submittable account already set up, as that's the most common submission portal used by publications. If you don't have one ahead of time you'll be able to create one the first time you run into a magazine requiring it.

Other items to consider are whether they've requested any changes to the standard manuscript format (SMF). This is a default format for story submissions, but not all editors want every aspect of it used for stories sent to them. They will specify what changes they'd like to see. Otherwise, submitting writers should always default to SMF. We'll discuss this more in Chapter Seven.

Read the guidelines carefully and make sure there aren't any special requests from the editor that don't fit the categories already mentioned. Examples of this would include those editors who prefer straight quotation marks instead of curly ones, those who don't want page numbers listed, or those who don't want any personally identifying information on the manuscript (meaning they don't want your name or contact information included, likely because they do blind submissions to ensure fairness in choosing stories.) These are only a few examples, so submitting writers should always keep their eyes peeled for any other special requests from the editors. Again, these requests are always for a reason, not to make your life more difficult, and they'll have specific applications.

Something you likely won't find on the submission guidelines is to be sure to remove any editing comments. If you've tracked changes or entered comments and shown markups, or if you've sent the story to someone else and they've done so, be sure to remove all those edits before turning your manuscript in. It's bizarre, as an editor, to get a document with the markups showing or with visible edits still in the manuscript. You'll find these settings under the "Review" tab of your Word document, in the "Tracking" box. It should be as simple as choosing "No Markup" in the relevant box, but double check to be sure it worked.

One big thing to keep in mind is that the editor's time should be respected. As writers, we want our time respected, as well, which to us means getting responses to our submissions within a reasonable time period or being allowed to submit to multiple publishers at the same time. We need to expect that editors also need a similar type of respect. The best way we can show editors respect is by reading all submission guidelines and following them. It's a small ask in the scheme of things. Chances are, if you plan to write more than one story for publication, you'll probably be submitting to the same editors more than once. Make sure they remember you as someone who follows the guidelines and not as someone whose appearance in the inbox makes them wish they hadn't shown up to work that day.

If an editor's desires aren't easily discernible, there are two other ways a writer can research what the editor is looking for. The big one is to read the publication they edit. Their tastes should be clear in the stories they've published in the past. Sometimes publishers will offer cheaper or free versions of the publication so people can do their research. Other publications publish their stories free online to begin with, which gives an easy leg up to writers looking to research in that way. Don't get me wrong, this doesn't mean you'll magically glean every aspect of an editor's taste from reading one issue. In fact, that's probably not going to happen. It will, however, show whether they like a literary flavor or a more laid-back writing style, whether they like a bit of humor or obviously don't, and what kind of subject matter and language has been allowed through.

The other way is to search online for interviews with the editor or editors you're planning on submitting to. Duotrope provides a link to their own interviews with editors when one is available. But many editors grant interviews for magazines, blogs, periodicals, and other publications that can help get their preferences and tastes out. In the end, sometimes you just have to swallow your fear and submit something you think works. The worst that can happen is a rejection, and you'll be getting plenty of those anyway, which we'll talk about more in Chapter Twelve.

CONCLUSION

The short version of this chapter is simply to respect the editor's time, your time, your story, and their wishes. Read the submission guidelines. Read them more than once. Make sure you've done what they've asked you to do, whether it concerns the content of the story or the way in which the story is submitted to them. The guidelines exist for a reason and breaking them won't do anyone any favors. Pushing back against guidelines isn't going to get a writer published, and it may guarantee that they aren't considered in the future. In your search for someone who loves your story the same way you do, it's vital to pay attention to what editors are looking for, and to stay on the neutral, if not good, side of the editors. Following their guidelines and requests is a simple way to do this.

CHAPTER SUMMARY

- Submission guidelines are vital to check before attempting to submit a story, and can be found on the publisher's website.
- Ensure your story matches the theme/genre.
- Ensure your word count is within the stated word count parameters.
- Ensure you don't submit when they are closed to submissions or between rolling deadlines or reading periods.
- Read through all the guidelines at least once thoroughly and follow any extra guidelines the editors have requested.
- Different publications will have different requirements.
- If no requirements are given, default to standard manuscript format.
- Pay attention to what they want in the cover letter and the subject line.
- Most prefer .doc submissions, but double check.
- Know whether to submit via email, mail, or a submission portal.
- Respect the editor's time.

CHAPTER 6
PERSONAL GUIDELINES & LEGAL CONSIDERATIONS

We've discussed the guidelines given to us by the editors, but what about your own guidelines or preferences? What should you be considering in terms of what is most favorable to you, your story, and your career before submitting? Editors aren't the only ones with an investment here. The writer should make sure they're happy with certain aspects of the market before submitting, rather than just blindly submitting.

CONTRACT TERMS

The big thing to consider would be the contract terms, but that won't always be made available in advance (though many publishers do either give you the contract terms on their submission guidelines page or even have an upload of their contract available to view). If the contract terms are provided in some way, make sure you're comfortable with them before you submit.

Two important elements to consider are the term of the contract and the rights they take. The term length tends to be drastically different between publishers, with one publisher only keeping the exclusive rights to a piece of work for one month and another keeping the rights for two years. While there are likely longer terms than two years somewhere, the longest I ever experienced was two years, and had it not been such a respectable magazine, I likely would have turned them down on that basis. That's a long time to allow someone else possession of your story and for it to be in limbo, unable to be used elsewhere.

In terms of rights taken, that's more complicated. First, to be clear, once you write a story, it is copyrighted. While there are additional steps that can be taken to officially copyright a piece, which includes a fee, you should be safely copyrighted once you've written it. Editors will be well aware of this, so there is no point in writing a copyright on your story before submitting it. They might actually surmise you're an amateur if you do so! The most common rights requested by publications in the U.S. are First North American Serial Rights. This means you are handing the publication the right to be the first to publish this piece in a North American serial publication (a magazine or periodical). There are other variations on the "first" publication, such as First Electronic Rights, First International Rights, etc. The term "first" is the important one here. This means you're guaranteeing that it has not been published elsewhere before, and they're the first to publish it. Violate that trust at your own risk. Be aware that these types of rights may be written in all manner of ways. Should you receive a contract with an unfamiliar type of rights, always, always, always look that term up, search for information on that publisher, and overall do your research to make sure you're comfortable with what they're asking for.

Something most wish to avoid is giving away All Rights. If it says All Rights in the contract, consider whether it's worthwhile for you to give away all variations on the rights being offered. This basically means you're signing your story over to them and have no right to publish it in any form (electronic, paper, audio, etc.) in the future. Personally, there'd have to be a hefty pay day for me to even pretend to consider giving away all my rights on a story. Any publication requesting these rights has shown they are unprofessional or don't actually know what they're doing. That, or they're predatory.

There are various forms of publication that may or may not be covered in the rights requested in a contract. The two most common are going to be print and electronic. Some publications only come out in electronic form, which is e-book or publication on their website, so they'll likely only ask for the electronic rights. If this happens, that means you can still sell the print rights elsewhere, but make sure that other publication *only* wants print rights (meaning on paper), because you cannot legally give them the first electronic rights, having sold those to another publication already.

A third type of rights is audio. This is for audiobook and podcast or formats of that ilk. This one is rarely taken by publishers with print and electronic unless they're trying to cover all their bases in case they might later consider doing an audiobook. There are several publications that only put out podcast versions of the story, most done by actors or the hosts of the show, but some give the author the option to read their own work for the recording. Still others give the author the choice. These podcast publications will typically solely take the audio rights, leaving the print and electronic rights to the author. As with most things, there are exceptions, so read the terms carefully.

Another element of this is the region in which the publisher holds the rights. A publisher taking only North American Rights can only publish that piece in the United States and Canada. They cannot turn around and publish the story in England without first gaining those rights from the author. If the publisher wants the rights for outside of North America, they must get International Rights via their contracts. Note that this information is for those living in North America only. For those living elsewhere, be sure to research the rights for your country or region before moving forward with any contract.

There are also Second Rights, Reprint Rights, or One-Time Rights, which are all usually applied to a reprint. That is, if a story has already been published once, most likely under First North American Serial Rights, it can be sold to other markets once the exclusivity period is over. So if a magazine, for example, asks for those First Rights for a period of six months, the story's Second Rights (or one of the other terms above) can be sold to a different periodical after six months. This is how "Best of" publications are put out. These publications will want to know where and when it was first published so they can give proper attribution.

Finally, they may ask for Archive Rights. This means that they have the right to keep the story, with non-exclusivity, on the format in which it was first published. So if a short story was published electronically and is accessible to viewers clicking through the site, while they no longer have the exclusive rights, they do have the right to not delete that file off their website. It is now considered archived on their site. Now you can do what you want with it, because you've got your own rights back.

PAY/HONORARIUM

Pay is a big factor and will be in the contract, but we're going to address it separately here. You should go into your submissions knowing how much you're willing to take for your story. There are levels of pay, and a publication will list that pay on their submission guidelines. Be wary if there's no mention at all. Even if they're not paying for the pieces they publish, that should be addressed on their submission guidelines page. For simplicity's sake, let's use Duotrope's definition of the pay scales:

- Token – This will pay less than $.01 per word and may just be royalty pay, a flat fee, or a contributor copy (meaning they send the author a copy of the book as their payment).
- Semi-Professional – This will pay $.01 to $.049 per word. This may also include royalty or a flat fee. The way to figure that out would be to do the math. Take the amount to be paid for the story (say, $100) and divide that by the number of words in your story (5000 words). This works out to be $.02 per word, which puts you squarely in semi-professional pay.
- Professional – This will pay more than $.05 per word. Again, this could include royalty or a flat fee, and the math would be done the same way.
- For the Love – This means no pay, no contributor copy. It may be referred to as being paid in exposure.

There are additional things to consider, some already mentioned above. If they're offering royalties, know that you may never see a penny. Royalties are typically paid out on any amounts received above the price of having published the story in the first place. If they're doing it that way, they will mention this in their submission guidelines. If that is not part of it, they're likely taking a share, or percentage, of the royalties while giving the rest to the authors. The way this would look on the submission guidelines or contract would be a percentage to be split between the authors. For example, a publisher may say that the authors will split forty percent of the royalties. They will hopefully say where the other sixty percent of royalties are going. Some give a portion of those to a charity, some take that percentage to pay toward their initial costs of publication, but either way, they should be transparent about what's happening with the income from the publication. There may also be a specific end period for the royalties. If not, expect that the royalties are ongoing into perpetuity, as long as the publication remains up for sale. I've seen a recent trend of publishers paying out royalties for a one-year period then paying those same royalties out to a charity after that contracted period.

Flat fees are just that—a specific dollar amount that will be paid out. This can cover a wide range of payments, from one dollar to $500. This may be paired with royalties, meaning the author will receive the flat fee, plus ongoing royalties for their contracted term. Contributor copies can also be combined with any of the above options; they aren't always given in lieu of payment, but rather in addition to payment. It's important to know whether the contributor copy will be electronic or print. An electronic copy costs nothing to give to the author, while there is a cost to the publisher to send a print copy. Some send a combination, and some will send more than one print contributor copy. All these should be addressed in the submission guidelines, which is why they exist to serve both the publisher and the author. This should all be in the contract.

In selecting pay, I like to aim for the top range first, then trickle down, so I'll look up pro publishers first and submit to them. If the pro publishers reject the story, semi-pro is next. So on and so forth. You may never know if your story is good enough to be accepted by the top publishers if you don't try. On the flipside of that, there are lower paying publications that may be perfect for a story, or there may be a publication that you want to work with, no matter what they pay. There are many things to consider when it comes to pay. Despite what I said about royalty payments above, there are publishers I've wanted to work with enough that I took that royalty contract, knowing full-well that I might not ever get paid for the story. This is always going to be up to the author's discretion. Others simply aren't comfortable submitting to higher paying publications until they're more confident in their writing, and that's fair, too. There is no wrong way to make this decision. Honestly, I've submitted to a magazine because they always had fantastic cover art and I wanted my story in one of those books with an awesome cover slapped onto it. Not every decision I make about the possible publication of a story will have to deal with cost.

Having said that, deciding what pay you'll take depends upon various factors, such as what your ultimate goal is. Is your goal simply to be published, no matter where? Is your goal the widest exposure possible? What about relationship building? Some of the best publishers I've worked with have been those who paid less for stories, but they were wonderful and easy to work with. Some of these publishers have become my friends. If you're looking to live off your stories, you definitely need to be aiming for higher pay or looking for self-publishing, which is an option we'll go over in a future chapter.

On a side note here, you should have a PayPal account set up before you start submitting to publications. The vast majority of short story publishers prefer to pay by PayPal. Be prepared to lose a percentage of your payment, as PayPal takes a bite out of payments sent through them. Consider this a cost of doing business. Those who don't pay via PayPal usually mail a check. I have yet to get a payment via check from a publisher.

REPUTATION

Another factor when choosing a publication is to consider how you feel about the publication itself. How do you feel about the tone used by the publishers? Have you seen how they treat people on social media? Are there complaints online? You will be working with these people for a specified time period, and just like any other working relationship, how you feel about them will matter. If a publisher comes across as harsh, judgmental, critical, or nasty on the publication's website or social media, chances are that's how they'll be when you're working with them. Does the website look professional? Are there typos all over it? Remember, the website quite possibly reflects the quality of the final product. If they cannot make sure their website—something that many will see first—looks professional and error-free, what does that say about the publications they put out?

Also look at past publications of the publisher you're considering. How do those look? Do they have amazing covers or ones that look cheap? If you can view the inside on a website like Amazon or in a bookstore, does it look professionally formatted or is it a mess? You're connecting your name with theirs when you publish with them, so be aware of what or who you're connecting with.

I post a monthly list of publishers looking for short stories, flash fiction, and poetry on my website, and that list always starts with this disclaimer: "I'm not endorsing these publications, merely passing them along. Always do your own due diligence before submitting." These words hold true here, too. By doing your own due diligence, I mean research the publication to your comfort level. If that simply means looking at the publisher's website, that's your choice. If that means, searching the internet, their social media, their print and e-books, and hiring a private detective, that's also your choice. Hopefully you find a nice comfortable place in between these two.

OTHER CONSIDERATIONS

Some other things to be aware of when you're looking at who to submit to are things like whether they take simultaneous submissions or multiple submissions, whether they take reprints, whether you have to query in advance, and what kind of publication it is. That last is the simplest. Is it a magazine, an anthology, or a standalone online publication? An anthology is a book full of short stories by various authors, as compared to a collection, which would be a single author gathering their own stories together into one publication. Some publishers publish each story on its own on their website. Others put each short story out on an app or as a single item on sites like Amazon and charge for the individual story.

We've already discussed reprints briefly, but why it matters here is if you're looking to sell a story you've already sold once. Some people keep submitting those old stories until they're tapped out in terms of publishers. Some pick their favorite stories and submit them to more publications as reprints. Others may not typically do this, but could see a call that fits an older story of theirs perfectly, so decide to submit it again. Whatever the reason, the author always needs to maintain transparency. This means only submitting to publications that state they take reprints and always putting in the submission that it is a reprint. Otherwise, you're deceiving the publisher into thinking they're getting the First Rights, and that's going to be a breach of contract and a legal issue. Sure, the chances of a publication coming after you are slim, but is that the type of person you want to be known as in the publishing world? Better to be ethical on your own.

It's important to note here that the vast majority of publishers count it as a reprint if it has already been published somewhere by you, including on a blog or website. If you sent your story out to newsletter subscribers, that counts, too. Entered it in a contest and they posted the winning entries on their website? Yep, that's a reprint then. It's pretty simple for publishers to do a search to see if the story's been made available to the public in some way, shape, or form. Don't forget that old pages could have been memorialized in screenshots or archives. There are probably many more ways a story could have been put out there that I'm not covering, but if you're not sure if your story is a reprint, query the publication. They usually have an email address for queries, and if not, send your query to the submissions email. Better to be safe than sorry.

When I say simultaneous submission, I'm referring to submitting the same story to more than one market at a time. Some publishers will say they're okay with writers submitting to more than one market at a time, but they ask that writers let them know if they sell the story elsewhere. This isn't going to be a bidding war like occasionally happens with novels. Screw around with making publishers compete for a story and you're more likely to lose both offers of publication. While there are writers that will submit to multiple markets, despite the publishers asking to submit the story only to them during the reading period, this again comes back to your personal ethics. I choose to be ethical, because it matters to me, whether there's a chance they'd find out or not. Having said that, I've screwed up and accidentally submitted to two markets at once when at least one of them didn't take simultaneous submissions. Luckily, it never became an issue, but I would have been honest had something odd happened, like offers of publication from both parties.

Multiple submissions refers to a single market allowing writers to submit more than one story to them during an open call period or to a specific publication of theirs. There are some that will allow writers to submit two different stories for a call (usually not more than that), which is applicable if you have two stories that would work for a specific theme, for example, but you can't decide which one would be best for that market. If they're open to it, let them make that choice. Some, though very few, will even consider publishing more than one story by a single author in a single publication. This is more likely to happen with flash fiction and poetry than short stories. There are markets that will only allow multiple submissions if they're different formats, such as submitting a poem and a short story.

Some publications require that the writers query them about their story before submitting. This is rare for short pieces of fiction, but it does happen. They will sometimes give the specifications for these queries, but if they don't, the best tactic is to put together a brief description or synopsis of the short story, then send that information in with the genre, title, and word count. Again, default to whatever they stipulate in their instructions, but if there is no information other than to query, these are the items that should be included, at minimum. For short stories, it's not going to be a long query letter or synopsis as would be expected with a novel. It's just intended to tell them what the story is about and what the feel or flavor of it is.

If a publication charges for submission, I typically stay away from it. While there may be a perfectly good reason for them charging for submission, I view being a professional author as a job, which means I should be getting paid, not the other way around. There are plenty of people who disagree with me here; you may be one of them. If so, a few other things to consider if you're willing to pay the fee is whether you'll be paid upon publication, thus having the possibility that you'll get your money back if they accept your story; whether they're transparent about why they're charging a fee; whether the entry fee will in any way influence their publishing decisions (in which case, you're absolutely paying to get published); the respectability of the publication; and if it comes with feedback should you get rejected. Some publications that charge a fee for entry will have periods throughout the year where they'll offer a free entry. Often, this is because they know there are writers who are financially struggling, and they want to give them a chance at publication, too. Keep an eye out for those publications if you can't afford the entry fee. I've actually seen the entry fee with literary magazines more than with genre publications. It's up to you whether you're okay paying for the possibility of getting published.

These are just a few of the specifications that might influence your choices to submit to a single market. What it all boils down to is what you want to do and what your end goal is. Don't forget that you're forging a working relationship with a company, one that requires a contract, and that means reading all the information presented, doing research if that's something you think would be helpful or necessary, and being comfortable with everything involved in that relationship. A different way of looking at it is that you're agreeing to briefly work for a company. Treat it as you would any other professional working relationship.

CHAPTER SUMMARY

- If presented a contract in advance of submitting, make sure to read it thoroughly and only submit if you agree to the terms.
- Check for the rights the publication takes.
- Never give All Rights to a publisher.
- You can only give any sort of First Rights one time. After that it's a reprint.
- Make sure you're okay with the length of time they plan to keep the rights. Standard is up to a year.
- Most common rights taken in the U.S. are First North American Serial Rights.
- Each format has a set of rights (electronic, audio, print).
- Understand the pay (or lack thereof) before submitting.
- Be sure to have a PayPal account set up so you can be paid.
- Consider the reputation of the market before submitting.
- Know whether they take simultaneous or multiple submissions.

CHAPTER 7
WRITING CONTESTS

We now interrupt your regularly scheduled program to bring a brief chapter on writing contests. People ask about these all the time. The thing is, my opinion is pretty mixed on them. I've entered contests, I've run contests, and I've judged contests, so I come at this from multiple points-of-view.

In my opinion, writing contests are most valuable if you get feedback from them. If a writing contest isn't providing feedback, it might not be worth entering. If it's a highly respected contest where winning it would build your author credit, it's also possibly worth entering. Most writing contests have an entry fee, which can range from affordable to astounding. There are multiple reasons organizations or entities will charge for a contest:

- It's a portion of their annual income, especially with nonprofits
- They need to pay their judges
- The income is directly turned around and paid out as the prize money
- They're ripping you off

Determining where the money from your entry goes will help determine if it's worthwhile to enter. That can be hard to figure out without directly contacting the organization and asking what they do with the money. Most people aren't going to do that, and I'm not recommending it as a general rule. Some organizations will be transparent in their verbiage about the contest, which makes it easy. Most of the time, though, you're not going to know how the funds are being used. Note that if it's a non-profit, they have to make that information available, even if it's just by request.

Since you likely won't know exactly how the money is used, there are other things you'll need to look at to determine whether it's worthwhile. The reputation is important. If it's a small contest that no one has heard of and there's an entry fee, I'd recommend skipping this one. If it's a free contest that you want to enter just for fun, make sure you look through the terms they've made public so you're not submitting a manuscript to someone who might turn around and steal it in some way. One thing to consider in this case is how long they've been running this contest. If it's been running for years and there are no complaints online, it's probably safe. If it's a large contest that is run by a respected group or company, it's also probably safe. This has the bonus of looking good on cover letters and in bios. If you win a small, no-name contest, it's not going to boost your bio or cover letter unless there's nothing else to put in there.

Something else to consider is what you want out of the contest. If you want to have fun, that's an easy one to decide. If you want feedback, ensure the contest provides it. Some will charge additional for a critique, but those run by bigger writer's groups will often provide feedback throughout, even if they also charge extra for critiques. The critiques will be much more thorough and fleshed out. If you're looking to grow, my personal recommendation is to pay for the critique when it's offered, at least if you see the judges consist of actual published authors, editors, and agents. Finally, if you're looking to make money off the contest, you need to weigh whether the loss of the fee is worth the significantly smaller chance of winning. If the entry fee is more than the prizes, it's definitely not worth entering. If it's a healthy prize, with even third place being more than the fee, that's worth considering. At the same time, you may have a better chance with that story of getting paid to have it published versus winning one of three prizes. If you're going for a payday, it needs to be worth it.

The judges are another consideration. If the contest posts who the judges are, check them out. If they're not editors, agents, or published authors, it might not be worthwhile. If you're being judged by people who are as inexperienced as you are, what are you actually gaining? Not expertise. And not necessarily a win that works to your advantage. Sometimes a contest will have a set of VIP judges who do the final round after other judges have narrowed it down. That's also worthwhile if those VIP judges are bigger names or people with a lot of expertise.

No matter who the judges are, bear in mind that they're only human, and that they may not agree with each other. Respectable contests will make sure more than one set of eyes look over each entry. This means there must be at least two judges per entry. A contest that has operated long enough will have also figured out that they need to have a way to deal with it if each of those two judges are completely split on the entry. In other words, if one judge absolutely loves it and scores it high, but the other judge absolutely hates it and gives it a low score, a third judge must be brought in. The contest operators will then take the two most comparative scores and drop the outlier. If they don't work this way, the results could be deeply skewed. It does give some insight into how differently a single story can be viewed, though. It shows why one editor will reject it and another will love it and accept it for publication.

Another matter to consider is what they do with the entries. Some contests offer publication for the winners. Some contests will publish everyone who entered, even if it's just on their website. For the latter, I'd avoid it. That type of publication, with no pay, means you can't submit a short story to a paying market in the future. It's now been published. You've given up your chance to publish it elsewhere and get paid. For the former, consider what type of publication we're talking about. Will it just be published on their website? Is this an e-magazine where all their publications are posted online? If so, that's worth it. It means you've been paid to be published. Is it a writer's group that will be posting the stories online? Probably not worth it unless they run an actual publication.

Some publications will run their submission process as a contest, with only the top three getting paid for publication. In other words, it's not an actual contest. This is how they've chosen to be able to pay, rather than being a purely for-the-love market. I avoid these. While I understand it likely means this is a newer publication, and they might be working their way up to be able to pay all of their authors someday, it seems a little backhanded to me. If they're doing this *and* charging a fee, I say absolutely not.

When submitting to contests, make sure you follow their guidelines, just as you should be when submitting to paying markets. When I was running contests, it was astounding how few people bothered to read the guidelines or simply ignored them. If I had time, I would send it back, tell them to read the guidelines again, and allow them to resubmit. I was a volunteer, however, and didn't always have the time to do that, which meant they'd entered a paid contest and weren't eligible to win. They'd blown it, because they couldn't be bothered to read the very short, very simple guidelines. Don't be one of those people.

I realize that much of what I've said in this chapter is wishy-washy. The reason for this is that every contest is different. I therefore can't say to go for it every time with gusto, because some contests will not be legitimate. What I can tell you is what to check for, and to make the choice on your own based on what you can see of the contest guidelines. Many people who run contests mean well, but some don't. Always consider what you want to get out of it, what you *will* ultimately get out of it, and whether it's worth it for you. That's the most concrete thing I can tell you to do. Research the contest, look for any negatives posted online, see how long they've been doing it, check for their level of respectability, and go from there.

CHAPTER SUMMARY

- Not all contests are trustworthy. Research them.
- Determine what you want from a contest before submitting to it.
- Read the guidelines and follow them.
- Be careful about entering for-fee contests.
- Trustworthy and highly respected contests may look good on your cover letter/bio.

CHAPTER 8
SUBMISSION FORMATTING

Most publishers will note some of their specific requirements for formatting on the submissions page, but there is a default industry standard called Standard Manuscript Format. This is sometimes listed simply as SMF or even Shunn, due to William Shunn being the go-to source for SMF. For those who are already familiar with this formatting, you might want to skip this chapter, as I'll be going into how to proceed through these settings. The basics of SMF are as follows:

- Size 12 font
- Times New Roman or Courier New font
- Left-aligned
- Double spaced
- 1" margins all around
- First page starts one-third to one-half of the way down the page
- Page numbers on each page but the first
- Personal information at the top left of the first page
- Header on every page but the first that includes your last name and the title (or a portion of the title if it's a long one)

- Approximate word count at the top right of the first page (rounded to the nearest hundred)
- Title and byline (whatever name you write under—can be a pen name) on the first page
- Use #, centered, for scene breaks
- Only one space after a period (not technically Shunn, but required for formatting submissions)

Besides these basics, there are a few more requirements for most manuscript submissions, which I'll cover below with more in-depth information on the above list. These include making sure extra spaces aren't put between paragraphs, removing widow/orphan control so the pages come out even in length (otherwise, if there's only one sentence of a new paragraph, for example, Word may automatically put the entire paragraph, including that sentence, on the next page, which means the previous page is one sentence shorter than it should be), and automatically indenting paragraphs (hitting "tab" or, worse, hitting the space bar a bunch of times to indent paragraphs is a big no-no.)

Double spacing doesn't apply to the information at the top of the page. This section will usually include your name (your real name, not your pen name), your address, your phone number, and your email address. Sometimes a publisher will ask you to note your PayPal address here, too, in which case you can simply add "(PayPal)" next to your email address unless it's a different email. If your PayPal email address is different from your contact email, put the PayPal one underneath your contact email and put the parentheses next to it so they know that's the PP address for payment.

All of this information will be at the top left and will be single spaced. Some publishers find this to be old-fashioned, as it started when manuscripts were being mailed in, but most still require it. Those that don't want it will say so in their submission guidelines, so always default to this form (reminder: the PayPal address and note only go in this area if the publisher specifically asked for it—it's otherwise frowned upon). If they request blind submissions this information should be left blank instead. Blind submissions mean your name and any personally identifying information should be left off your manuscript, which will include the header that we'll address later in this section.

The word count, which again is rounded to the nearest hundred unless the publisher specifies otherwise, will go on the top right, which can be accomplished by tabbing over from the end of your name. It should simply say, "About x00 words." That's it. If the publisher asks for an exact word count here, you would honor their request, rather than rounding it up. When they ask for the exact word count, that is the body of your story only, not your information at the top and not the title and byline.

Sample of standard manuscript format (Shunn)

BODY FORMATTING

*The following instructions are for Microsoft Word 365, specifically. Other forms of Word should have similar settings, but they may be slightly different.

Let's talk font first. To set the size and type of the font, there will usually be a display on your toolbar at the top of Microsoft Word on the "Home" tab. The simplest way is to use the drop-down menu in these windows to set the fonts. If not, there is a "Design" tab that has a "Fonts" pulldown menu. You can also open a specific window for font control by clicking on the diagonal arrow in the bottom right portion of the toolbar; this is referred to as the Font Dialog Box Launcher. This will give you access to more settings options for the font.

To double space your document, refer to the "Paragraph" square on the toolbar on the "Home" tab (usually directly next to the "Font" tab). Click the Paragraph Dialog Box Launcher. Here we're going to do a few things addressed above. There are two tabs in this dialog box, one called "Indents and Spacing" and one called "Line and Page Breaks." We'll hit the I&S tab first, under the "General" section. In the "Alignment" box, make sure it says "Left." Otherwise, use the drop-down menu to select it. "Outline Level" should remain "Body Text." This means your sentences will be evenly aligned on the left side of the page, but jagged, or uneven, on the right.

Under the "Indentation" section the only thing you should need to touch is on the right, under "Special." Here, click on the drop-down menu and select "First line." Then, under "By" select ".5." This will automatically indent the beginning of each paragraph by one-half inch. Publishers may ask for a different default amount, in which case you'd enter that instead. I usually do this after I've typed in the title and byline, as those need to be double spaced, but they'll be centered instead of indented in any way. Note that the "Left" and "Right" sections should remain at 0, and "Mirror indents" should *not* be checked.

Next, on the same tab, but under the "Spacing" section, you're once again working with the selections to the right of that space. Under "Line Spacing" select "Double." Leave the "At" selection blank. Make sure "Before" remains at 0, but Word should have already defaulted "After" to "8pt." Here, you will also check the box underneath that says "Don't add space between paragraphs of the same style." If this box is not checked, there will be an extra space between paragraphs. A lot of submissions come in this way for beginners, and it marks the writer as exactly that. It's more professional if your manuscript is correctly formatted, so don't let this one slip under the wire.

Sample Paragraph dialogue box

Note that for the double spacing and space between paragraphs portion of these instructions, it's easiest to do that after you've entered your personal information on the top left, but before typing in the title and byline. So I usually do the double spacing after I type in my personal information, hit "enter" until I'm about halfway down the page, temporarily center the page instead of having it left-aligned (which can be done in the toolbar by clicking the appropriate set of lines), type in the title, hit "enter," type in my byline (By Shannon Lawrence, as I don't use a pen name), hit "enter" twice, then go back into the Paragraph Dialog Box and do the First Line Indent settings. Others go back and do all the formatting after they've completely finished the story. I've found it's easier for me to prepare my page right from the beginning so that once I get past the title and byline, everything flows as its supposed to and I don't have to try to fix things afterward. You might find it easier to do it all after. This is completely up to you. There's no wrong or right time to do it (aside from before you submit it, of course). For me, seeing the page all nicely set up tells my brain it's go time, and I start typing away. It's now become part of my routine.

Now we go to the "Line and Page Breaks" tab, where the only thing you should have to do is click the box next to "Widow/Orphan control." This will fix the problem of possible uneven pages, and can be done at any time before you submit the story.

For margins, click on the "Layout" tab on your main toolbar. There will be a "Margins" drop-down menu in the "Page Setup" section. Simply click on the arrow and select "Normal," which should specify one-inch margins all around (top, bottom, left, right). This will ensure the white space is even all around the text on the page. That is, until the appropriate header is added for the identification and page numbers.

PAGE NUMBERS/HEADERS

That takes us to the last major setting on the manuscript. To add the page number and personally identifying information in the header, go to the "Insert" tab on the main toolbar. About three-quarters of the way to the right, there will be a "Header & Footer" section. Click on the arrow next to "Page Number," then put your cursor over "Top of Page," which will have its own drop-down menu. From this menu, the best selection is usually called "Plain Number 3." If this title is not present, select the simple version that shows a number on the right side. Once this is clicked, it will open up space to type at the top of the page. Here, type "Last Name/Title/" before the actual page number. You should notice that the toolbar has also changed. Once you've typed this information in, go back up to the toolbar and click the box by "Different First Page." This will make sure the page numbers start on the second page with the number two, and that the name and title don't appear on that first page, either, since your identifying information is already there. Hit the red X to close this, and it will put the previous toolbar back and close the writing space in the header.

FINISHING UP

After you've jumped through these hoops, your manuscript is formatted! That is, if the publisher didn't ask for changes to SMF. If they asked for changes or have specific formatting requirements, you'll have to make those requested changes. If someone wants something significantly different from SMF, I usually save that as a new document and make the changes there. Otherwise, if I were to get a rejection I'd have to go back into the original document and change it all back. Easier to just have that other version to turn in, then delete it or file it once it's turned in. There's no way I could possibly cover every eventuality when it comes to publisher requests, but a few I've seen are things like changing the curly quotes to straight quotes, using a different font style or size, not indenting the manuscript at all (so using the type of formatting more common in emails, where there are no indents and there are instead spaces between paragraphs), or single spacing. There are as many variations as there are publishers, so here's your regular reminder to...what? Always read the submission guidelines.

CHAPTER SUMMARY

- Standard Manuscript Format is Shunn formatting, and is the default.
- Some basics of SMF are 12 font, Times New Roman/Courier New, double spaced, title and byline centered 1/3 to 1/2 of the way down the page.
- Round word count to nearest hundred and put at top right of first page.
- Put title, author last name, and page number as header on all but first page.
- Always read the submission guidelines for any changes or extras to the formatting.

CHAPTER 9
BIO

This is as good a time as any to consider your bio. Most publications are going to ask for one, whether they ask you to submit it on your cover letter (which we'll cover in the next chapter) or they request it after they've accepted your story. It's expected that authors have at least two versions: a long version and a short version. The short version should be no more than 100 words. The long version should be no longer than 200 words. I would also personally recommend having a micro-version, especially if you'll be speaking at events, conferences, conventions, or other appearances, as they use these to introduce you at the beginning of your workshop and it can become tiring to hear repeatedly.

A bio is a personal thing, so all I can offer are some basic guidelines and recommendations. Consider the tone you want your bio to take. Should there be a touch of humor or should it be dry? If you write in only one genre or have a primary genre, the bio should be geared toward that genre. As you publish and move through the writing world, the bio will most likely morph along with your career. A creative bio stands out to publishers and audience members alike, so consider throwing something entertaining into the mix, especially in a longer version. In addition, consider an aspect of your personality or hobbies that might make you sound more interesting.

Having said all that, the first rule of bios is that they need to be in third person. A bio starting, "I write horror" is going to show people you're an amateur. A good way to start a bio is with your name (your pen name, if you have one). That ensures your name is the first thing they see, and it also sets the bio as being in third person. At the beginning, you might not have any publications credits, and that's okay! Publishers aren't typically going to toss a submission because they don't see previous writing credits listed. In fact, some publishers only take unpublished writers. And others will occasionally have issues dedicated to unpublished writers. Who doesn't want to be the person to discover the Next Big Name in fiction? Aside from that, many publishers are published or aspiring authors, and they want to give others an opportunity to get published, too. The writing community can be a caring and supportive one.

If you do have publishing credits, include no more than three in your bio. If there are more publication credits than those two or three you choose to list (I usually only list two), that can be indicated in the bio by saying something like, "John Doe has published stories in magazines and anthologies, including x and y." Or "John Doe has published in x, y, and several other publications." The wording is up to you, but it gives you an idea. As far as which publications to select, the more respected or higher paying ones should be mentioned. So if you have two pro-paying sales under your belt, you should certainly include those two in your bio. Unless one of those is an anthology, and that anthology might not be well known. In which case, it is sometimes best to err on the side of choosing any pro-paying magazines you were published in instead. Anthologies can be more obscure to other publishers than magazines that have been around long enough to be coughing up professional rates, as an anthology could easily be a one-off. Also, if you submit different genres, it might make sense to switch out the publications to whatever's most relevant to what you're submitting. So if you're submitting a mystery, you'll want to put on there that you've been published by *Ellery Queen*, but if you're submitting horror, your number one should be *Nightmare Magazine*. You're presenting them an image of yourself and what type of writing you've sold in the past. You're also telling them which of their fellow editors have liked your work.

Another thing to consider including in a bio is any expertise or degree that might have bearing on your writing. If you write stories about the Loch Ness Monster and are a registered cryptozoologist, it makes sense to mention that in a bio. If you have a degree in History and write historical fiction, that should be mentioned. And if you have an MFA, by all means slot that in. This can apply to esteemed writing programs, as well. If you've gone through something like the Odyssey Writing Workshop, that's worth mentioning. Also worth including is if you've won any contests or awards having to do with your writing, or if you belong to a respected writer's group, such as SFWA (Science Fiction and Fantasy Writers of America) or the HWA (Horror Writers Association). These are all options that might look good in a bio and possibly catch someone's eye, but again, if you don't have any of these things, that's okay, too. Focus instead on making what you do want to say interesting. Everyone has to start somewhere.

If you do something art related or your job is of interest or just something you want to mention, that can be included, too. For example, if you also sell photography or artwork, that can be mentioned. If you work a day job that pertains to your writing style, such as a police officer writing mysteries, that's something that lends credence to your writing. Be careful about including something in an attempt to sell readers on a product or service you charge for, as that could be off-putting to them. For example, if you sell Mary Kay, this isn't the place to refer people to your Mary Kay website. Same goes for if you sell life insurance, which doesn't mean you can't mention what your day job is in your bio if that's what you want to do, but don't put your life insurance sales website in your bio. The only website in your bio should be the one to your author website, if you have one, or something along those lines. You want people to want to seek you out and find other things you've written. I detail what you need to know about an author website in Chapter Twenty.

Yet another thing you might want to include is if you're part of a marginalized community, plus your pronouns if they're relevant.

Marginalized communities might include writers who are non-white, female writers, writers with disabilities, or writers who are LGBTQ+. Pronouns can either be referenced in their own space or can be worked into the third person bio. Now more than ever, publishers are seeking diversity in the voices they publish. It's also a good idea if you write pieces that address the communities you belong to. It lends that much more credence to what you've written and makes it so no one gets upset about appropriation. Personally, I choose not to mention that I'm Native American and disabled, *unless* I am submitting a story that specifically covers issues for these communities. I do not want to be published *because* I belong to one of these communities; I want to be judged on my work only. However, I also want to make it clear, when relevant, that I am a part of the community I'm writing about, so that it doesn't come across as disrespectful. Notice in my bios below that I simply mix my pronouns into the rest of the bio, but either way is good.

If all else fails, people love animals. Mention your cats, your dogs, your birds, or your other pets. Say something funny or clever about them. In my long bio, I mention my minions (my kids) and my familiars (my cats). Some people choose to mention their kids—though I'd recommend never giving out their names—their spouses or significant others, and where they live (in general, not their actual address). It all comes down to what you're comfortable sharing and what you want people to know about you. For the most part, I don't mention my kids or my husband, because I feel that's private.

Consider keeping a document in your writing folder that has all your bios so you can easily copy/paste them into the necessary places when they're requested. Writing a new bio every time is a waste of time and can cause undo stress. Unless, of course, your thing is being spontaneous, in which case I say to have at it. Like most other things I'm going over, you decide where to stick to the rules and how you run your own writing career. I'm here to help you lay the groundwork so you can hopefully excel and move right on past me, and I can be like, "I knew them when," though not really, because you buying this book doesn't necessarily mean I know you. Ah, well.

Now that we've gone over those ground rules, I'll give you my bios as examples. Hopefully you'll see that I've tried to add a slightly creepy tone, but also shown that I have a sense of humor. I've also squeaked in mention of my podcast and a couple of my personal hobbies (hiking and photography), which seemed more interesting than shrugging and telling people I'm a mom of two and I write things.

Micro: Shannon Lawrence writes primarily horror and fantasy, with stories published in magazines and anthologies. She's also a true crime podcaster. She can be found at www.thewarriormuse.com.

Short: A fan of all things fantastical and frightening, Shannon Lawrence writes primarily horror and fantasy. Her short fiction can be found in over forty anthologies and magazines, including Space and Time Magazine and Dark Moon Digest. You can also find her as a co-host of the podcast Mysteries, Monsters, & Mayhem. When she's not writing, she's hiking through the wilds of Colorado and photographing her magnificent surroundings, where, coincidentally, there's always a place to hide a body or birth a monster. Find her at www.thewarrior-muse.com.

Long: A fan of all things fantastical and frightening, Shannon Lawrence writes in her dungeon when her minions allow, often accompanied by her familiars. She writes primarily horror and fantasy. Her stories can be found in several anthologies and magazines, and her collections, Blue Sludge Blues & Other Abominations, Bruised Souls & Other Torments, and Happy Ghoulidays are available in stores. You can also find her as a co-host of the podcast Mysteries, Monsters, & Mayhem. When she's not writing, she's hiking through the wilds of Colorado and photographing her magnificent surroundings. Though she often misses the Oregon coast, the majestic and rugged Rockies are a sight she could never part with. Besides, in Colorado there's always a place to hide a body or birth a monster. What more could she ask for? Find her at thewarriormuse.com or mysteriesmonstersmayhem.com.

Note that I already broke one of my own suggested guidelines, which is to say that I only started one of my bios with my name. I like the flow of it the way I wrote it better, so I went with it. This is something you make your own because it's going to be the only thing other than your story representing you. This is meant to be who you want publishers and readers to know you as. A snapshot. And while these are my main ones, I also have some geared more toward mystery, humor, and the other types of work I've turned in, because I don't only write horror and fantasy. Not only that, but I remove reference to my collections when I'm asked to include my bio in my cover letter, but add them in when I'm presenting at a conference. My reasons for this are personal. I want editors to see who else has published me, rather than the books that are mine alone.

One more thing to consider is that there's no requirement to be honest. I don't mean you should lie about where you've been published. I'm instead referring to personal information you choose to share. I have several friends who like to randomly make up bios that say they do things like train circus clowns or travel as top-secret spies, or whatever else might have struck their fancy when preparing that bio for submission. If you do this, it's best to make the tone of the entire bio tongue-in-cheek or humorous so it's clear you're making things up. Many of you will be writing fiction, so why not utilize that skill in your bio?

Finally, it's a good idea to make tweaks depending upon the audience. By this I mean if I'm going to be speaking at an event with mostly elderly people, such as a library, I'll keep the bio simpler and more professional. If I'm speaking at a horror convention, I'll punch up the horror aspects. If I'm speaking at a professional writing conference, I might also default to a more professional bio, though that might also depend upon what workshops I'm teaching at that particular conference.

If you have trouble writing your bio, you might ask a friend to help by writing one for you. You could also do this as an exchange, where you write theirs and they write yours. Once you see what they felt was important enough to include in your bio, you can tweak it however you need. It does sometimes help to have someone who lives outside your head point out what matters or what they see. You can also try writing your own bio but having a friend tweak it. Use whatever method works for you.

There are a lot of factors to consider, and people often find it hard to write about themselves. Keep it short, keep it fairly simple, but also try to make it interesting and/or entertaining. Most of all, make it the reflection of yourself that you want people to see. This might be your first impression on a prospective reader.

CHAPTER SUMMARY

- Publications will often require your bio, as will event organizers.
- Have at least one short and one long bio. You might also want a micro bio.
- Bios should always be in third person.
- If you have publishing credits, include up to three in your bio.
- Consider including any expertise, education, or relevant group membership that impacts your writing knowledge.
- Include the URL to your website.
- Aim to inform and entertain.

PART FOUR
SUBMISSION TIME

What to Expect:

- Cover letters
- Submitting
- Keeping track of submissions
- Handling rejections
- Rewrite requests
- Acceptances
- Contracts
- Edits
- Withdrawing stories

CHAPTER 10
COVER LETTER

The cover letter, for the most part, is probably the least important aspect of a short story submission. Some editors say they don't even read it until after they've read the story. Some ask you not to do one. However, others do read it and even have their own specifications for requirements. With it being such a mixed bag, it's still an important enough element to consider and to construct correctly.

The first thing to do, of course, is check the submission guidelines for anything required in a cover letter. While I'm going to give a basic default version of a cover letter, the default is what you should use if there are no editor requests for what to include. Their request trumps the default, just as with formatting. The most frequently requested items are title, word count (usually the rounded estimate that is on the top of the manuscript), genre, a brief author bio or biographical statement, a brief publication history, and the author's contact information.

Some will also ask for a one-to-two-sentence synopsis. If so, this should be a quick summary of the plot that makes it sound interesting. This synopsis is intended to get the editor to give it a read instead of passing over it. Here, it's a good idea to run the synopsis by someone else if you're unsure as to how good it is. This synopsis may also end up being used by the publisher to advertise the book if the story does get accepted, so it's not just the editor/publisher who needs to be intrigued by it. It also must be usable if the story is accepted.

Example Synopsis: A heartbroken mother makes an ill-fated wish on a monkey's paw, but is she willing to the pay the price? *The Monkey's Paw*, by W.W. Jacobs.

As far as a default cover letter, it needs to be brief. This is nothing like a novel query. A default cover letter is often a summary of aspects of the manuscript (*not* the story), such as the items listed above as being requested by editors (word count, story title, genre, publication history, biographical information, and contact information). It should be five to six sentences or less and contain all that information. Below is an example:

> *Dear Editor,*
>
> *Squiggly Things is a horror short story of about 3500 words.*
>
> *I've had short fiction published in magazines and anthologies, including X Magazine and Y anthology. I am an HWA member. My website is www.squigglythingsauthor.com.*
>
> *Thank you for your consideration.*
>
> *Sincerely,*
>
> *Shannon Lawrence*
>
> *Address*
>
> *Phone number*
>
> *Email address*

Notice that most things fit into two sentences here. There doesn't have to be a different sentence for each piece of information. The first sentence addresses the genre, title, and length. The second sentence, in its own paragraph, addresses the biographical information. If you're part of a group that might lend credence to your place as an author, that should be included (HWA member reference in the example.) If it's not relevant, it shouldn't be included.

If the submission guidelines ask for an actual bio, the short bio that should have already been formulated before submission should be used instead of the biographical statement above. If you have a website, that should be part of your bio, and will therefore still be addressed.

A lot of this information is repetitious, right? The manuscript, unless otherwise requested, already has the title, word count, contact information, etc. Part of this is simply left over from when manuscripts had to be mailed in, but it's lived on in the emails. While I've heard a couple editors say it's ridiculous to include contact information under the signature, most still expect it. Consider if you're turning in a manuscript where the submission guidelines have requested no identifying information on the manuscript itself. The only place they'd find that information is in the email cover letter. Either way, it doesn't hurt to include the information, so it might as well be part of the default.

Notice also that the story itself did not get summarized. This should never be done unless specifically requested. In fact, it will sometimes be mentioned in submission guidelines with a request *not* to send a synopsis or any type of summary of the story. In other words, don't stress about creating a short story synopsis until you're actually asked to do so. Sending it in when not requested to do so may make you look like an amateur.

The opening line of the letter can be a sensitive issue. It used to be the default was Mr. Editor Name or Ms. Editor Name. In fact, it wasn't that long ago. But with more education come changes, and editors are as diverse a group of people as writers. It's important to be as inclusive as possible and respect an editor's pronouns and proper form of address. In order to determine the proper greeting, you should do at least some minimal research into the editor of the publication. If their bio uses he/his and she/her, it's probably reasonable to use the more traditional form of address (Mr. or Ms. and their last name.) However, if the editor uses different pronouns, there are two general options: use Mx. Editor Name or simply use their full name (Dear John Doe). Either one of those works. Unless I see something specifically saying Mx. is preferred as the standard form of address, I typically default to using the full name.

But there's another set of complications. Sometimes the editor isn't easily found. If you have exhausted the submission guidelines page, looked for an About Us/Masthead or similarly titled page, and overall scoured the publication's website looking for who the mysterious editor even is without finding anything, the final step before giving up and writing "Dear Editor" is to do an internet search. Sometimes a recent interview with that publication's editor will show up online, or someone will have written something about the publication that mentions the editor. If so, it's fairly safe to use that name for the greeting. If it's a really old article, it might be best to default to "Dear Editor," as there might have been a changeover in editors by now. If you're uncomfortable or doubtful about your information or how to address the editor, writing "Dear Editor" shouldn't be problematic. It's a fair default when the information isn't available.

The other complication is finding that there are a billion editors on the publication, making it tricky to figure out who to address. While there may be no perfect answer to this, it's typically safest to default to using the name of the managing editor as the greeting. In addition, if there's a specific short story or fiction editor (fill in whatever genre or type you're submitting here) mentioned, I'll include them in the greeting. While chances are that magazines or other publishers have unnamed slush readers looking at the incoming submissions before the named editors ever get a gander, it's best to be polite and show you did your homework and at least tried honestly to determine who you were submitting to. Editors get so many submissions written with a greeting to an editor at a different publication or that even have the name of a different publication in the title in some way that it may go a long way to see that you at least tried and that you were intending to submit to them, not someone else. The people who submit to incorrect names such as in the examples mentioned are showing they copy/pasted a cover letter from another submission and didn't even care enough to change it. This isn't the best way to get published. In addition, sending one email to multiple recipients is a bad idea. In other words, don't use a single email to submit to different markets. It should be one email per market. No one wants to be treated as just another number, and it's deeply disrespectful.

The vast majority of publishers make their editor information easily available, and it's rare to not be able to find something about the editor. For those that aren't available, maybe they simply didn't think about it, because the cover letter doesn't make or break anything for those specific editors, and they didn't figure someone would be stressing out about not knowing their name. All we writers can do is to try our best and default to something that's respectful if we can't find the information.

Just as with the synopsis, be wary of putting way too much information in a cover letter or acting cocky. For example, having seen many a goofy or unprofessional cover letter posted on social media by editors who've reached their limit, don't say you're the next Stephen King or that you're better than J.K. Rowling. All the cover letter is meant to do for most editors is cover the basic bits of information so they don't have to open an attachment if they're seeking the data. Instead, it's right there in the cover letter, and if they print up stories or read them on their e-book readers while going through slush, they can easily match the information between the cover letter and the manuscript in order to reply to the right person.

One important note to include here is to always bear in mind that an editor is a human being just like you. This is a symbiotic relationship. Editors need stories and writers who don't wish to solely self-publish need editors and publications. If we all need each other, it stands to reason that being polite and doing our best to respect the other party will encourage better relationships all around. Editors have to understand that writers will occasionally slip up and submit something incorrectly and writers have to understand that editors may not have covered all the bases yet.

Maybe you saw this coming, but reading the submission guidelines will often go a long way to keeping this symbiotic relationship in good working shape. Take a moment and read those puppies one more time before moving forward with your submission. Things can be missed or forgotten, especially with the length of some submission guidelines. Often, these lengthy guidelines exist because so many people ignore them in the first place. I've even seen a publication that wrote something in the middle of the guidelines page that had to be included in the email so they'd know if the submitter had bothered reading them all the way through. Editors get hundreds upon hundreds of submissions in a week, if not thousands, and it is easy for them to start to feel rundown by the people who ignore their requests. Looking at it from the outside, it's a pretty simple set of requests. At least it is most of the time.

CHAPTER SUMMARY

- Cover letters for short story submissions are meant to be short and simple.
- Cover letters differ per publication, so check the submission guidelines.
- Don't synopsize your story in the cover letter unless it's requested.
- Most commonly expected items in a cover letter are title, word count, genre, brief biographical statement, brief publication history, and the author's contact information.
- Pay attention to the editor name and their pronouns when addressing the letter or default to "Dear Editor."

CHAPTER 11
DOING THE DEED

Okay, here we are. Your story has been polished until it gleams. It has been formatted exactly as requested by your chosen publisher. The cover letter is written and you have a lovely and entertaining bio. There are just a couple more steps before you send your baby off into the big, wide world and await its judgment and future.

Are you ready for it? Yep. Check the submission guidelines one more time.

Now, from those guidelines determine how the publication wants the story submitted. If they have a form on their website, they'll have a link. If you go to that link and it says they're not taking submissions, even though the magazine is supposed to be open for submissions year-round, that typically means the submission platform they use is full for the month. If that's the case, you'll have to wait for the beginning of the next month. It costs a certain amount of money to take a specific number of submissions each month, so some magazines will have a cap at which they close submissions until the following month. For those magazines, your best bet is to submit within the first week of the next month.

Instead, you've clicked on the link that takes you to wherever and however they want you to submit, and now you're faced with a bunch of boxes to fill in. You should already have all that information sitting in front of you. These forms usually ask for the very same things we beat to death in the last chapter: genre, story title, word count, author email address, cover letter, bio, etc. Pay attention to any notes on this form that might differ from what was on their submission guidelines or may not have been covered there. If it just says "word count," for example, that's typically the rounded word count you've defaulted to elsewhere. Some will ask for the exact word count, though, because they pay per word and they'll go by your original word count before any edits they request. It's all about not rushing and just ensuring you submit things as necessary.

Some of these forms will want the story pasted into a box, while most will prefer it as an attachment just as would happen with an email. For the ones that want it pasted, they may have additional stipulations, such as putting underscores on either side of words or phrases that are meant to be italicized (so it would look like "You _absolute_ peach!" instead of "You *absolute* peach!). These and other stipulations concern how that manuscript will appear on the other end once put through the form. If you're attaching a document at their request, all those requests would typically have been made in advance in the submission guidelines. Publications will stress the type of document that can be accepted via these forms (.doc, .docx, .pdf, .txt). Most accept .doc as at least one of the options, which makes that a good format to default to whenever you're saving a document for the first time. To save as a .doc, choose the "Word 97-2003 Document" option in the pull-down menu.

Double check your information then hit that final "send" button. Some of these forms will require a box be checked that says terms of service or other guidelines have been read and understood. If so, that's usually right above the final send button, and the form will not send until it's checked. Sometimes these boxes ask you to confirm you're the original creator of the work or that it hasn't been published elsewhere. Make sure whatever's there has been read or is true, and that you're comfortable with it. Then hit that button to send your work.

If they want the manuscript emailed to them, it's time to open your email browser and find the email address they want the manuscript mailed to. Once that information is entered, it's time to see if they want anything specific written in the subject line. If nothing is mentioned about the subject line, it's usually a good idea to write something simple, but identifying, such as "Short Story Submission-Your Last Name" or "Short Story Submission-Title." This gives them an easy reference or identifier when they're moving through the hundreds of emails in their inboxes.

Okay, the email address and subject line are filled out. Now it's time to put that lovely cover letter in the body of the email, attach the document in the format they've requested, and send that email out. It's really quite simple once you've hit this point. Now your baby is in the wild, but there's more to do.

CHAPTER SUMMARY

- Check the submission guidelines before sending your story. Yep, one more time.
- Ensure you're submitting correctly (via email or submission portal).
- Check whether they want it sent as an attachment or pasted in the body of the email.
- Most publishers prefer .doc.

CHAPTER 12
KEEPING TRACK/DOCUMENTING SUBMISSIONS

I t's important to keep track of submissions in one way or another. This helps avoid awkward things like submitting the same story twice to a market accidentally. If you're only submitting one story at any given time, it may not seem worth it to keep track, but bear in mind that stories can be out for a long time, and it can be easy to lose track over time. Especially if the story ends up being on submission for months or years.

PLATFORMS

How you keep track is completely up to you. There are multiple ways to do so, some simpler than others. One is by using submission trackers, such as Duotrope and Submission Grinder. Not only do they provide a way to look up publishers, but they also provide a tracking system that allows writers to enter information about their submissions. There's a convenient page where all stories on submission can be pulled up. This page shows the story, the market, how long the piece has been on submission, how long pieces are typically on submission before a response is received, and some other items that you may or may not find helpful. In addition, when a publication is pulled up, the bottom of the publication's page will show the stories that writer has submitted (assuming they've reported them to the submission tracker), when they were submitted, and what the result was (or if it's still pending). There's also a way to see what their responses have been over the last month, which means someone can loosely track if a story of theirs has been out way longer than the average, and is therefore likely being considered. There are plenty of other bells and whistles, as well, which can be discovered by checking out one of the websites. There are also new versions popping up all the time. Some are paid services, but not all of them.

SPREADSHEET

Personally, while I also use one of the services (the better to stalk the last month's responses to see if I'm getting close to a response or if my story is maybe being considered), I keep a personal spreadsheet. This spreadsheet has multiple tabs, the first one being any stories currently on submission. The columns are for the date submitted, the publication, a link to the submissions guideline page, the story, the type of story (whether it's a short story, flash fiction, novella, etc.), and any notes I want to keep track of, such as what the query period is or if the story has been short listed. As not all publications are listed in the submission platforms, I'll also make a note if I found the publisher another way. At the bottom of the page, I keep a running list of anything that needs to be resubmitted after a rejection, or upcoming publications opening to submission and what story I want to submit while they're open.

Sample of Pending Submissions tab of spreadsheet

The second tab is for acceptances. I keep track of the date of acceptance, the publication date, the amount of pay contracted, and when the rights are returned in full after the contracted term. For this last, I initially put the date the contract ends, and once I reach that date, I remove the date and simply type CLEAR. Once I use that story in a personal collection, it will be grey highlighted so I know not to put it in a future collection. I also highlight stories that received pro pay, so I can keep track for professional organizations that require a minimum number of pro sales for full membership, such as The National League of American Pen Women or the Horror Writers Association. Any payments not received are highlighted in a different color so I can pursue payment if needed. Other items it would be worthwhile to keep on this page would be buy links for the book or magazine once it comes out, pricing of the publication once released, and any links or codes for purchasing author copies via the publisher.

Date	Submitted To	Website	Title	Type	Acceptance	Pub Date	Contract Term	Clear?	Pay	Received?
5/30/2021	Magazine of Undead Things	www.magazineofundeadthings.com	Pythons	Flash	6/5/2021	6/10/21	6 months	CLEAR	$30	$30
6/5/2021	Creepy Tribunal	www.creepytribunal.com	Monkey Soles	Short	7/1/2021	7/20/2021	90 days	CLEAR	$5	$5.00
4/20/2021	Fiction for the Shower	www.fictionfortheshower.com	Splish Splash	Flash	6/20/2021	7/1/2021	3 months	CLEAR	$4	$3.00
7/22/2021	Spikes in Brains	www.spikesinbrains.com	Lobotomy	Short	7/23/2021	8/1/2021	12 months	8/1/2022	$200	No

Qualifies for HWA 5.05 c/word
Payment pending
Never received payment

Sample of the Acceptances tab of spreadsheet

The third tab is for rejections. This is the original entry cut and pasted from the first tab, but with the date of rejection added, whether it was a personal or form rejection, and any comments from the publisher. There will be more on this in Chapter Twelve.

Date	Submitted To	Website	Title	Type	Date Rejected	Notes
8/31/2021	Haunted Animals	www.hauntedanimalsarefbo.com	Attack of the Ladybugs	Form	10/14/2021	
10/12/2021	Gone to Seed Magazine	www.seedlings.com	Rooting of the Dandelion	Personal	10/15/2021	Doesn't fit, but please send more
10/4/2021	Modern Day Horror	www.modernhorror.com	Secrets & Popsicles	Form	10/24/2021	
9/23/2021	Two Toads Quarterly	www.twotoads.com	A Skunk Among Us	Personal	10/22/2021	Loved it, but can't make it fit
9/12/2021	Recess Magazine	www.playtime.com	Seesaw From Hades	Form	11/3/2021	

Sample of the Rejections tab of spreadsheet

The fourth tab is for any other type of result. For example, if a magazine goes under before I get a response, I'm not going to consider that a rejection, so it goes on the "Other" tab with the date I realized the magazine had shut down and any notes on why this entry is on the "Other" tab. Additional items I might put on this tab include a story I pulled for another reason, such as the story being a simultaneous submission and selling to the other market. This tab doesn't get used much.

Date Sub	Title	Website	Story	Type	Reason Pulled/Date
3/15/2021	Liquid Sunshine	www.liquidsunshine.com	Raindrops on Roses	Short	Magazine closed 5/9/21
3/19/2021	On Track Magazine	www.ontrack.com	Trains & Cryptonite	Flash	Magazine closed 4/30/21
3/20/2021	Unthinkable Snails	www.unthinkable.com	Ratings Drop	Short	Switching formats to online only - withdrawn 5/15/21
5/24/2020	Peggy Pants Literary	www.peggypants.com	Sweet n Sour Gumballs	Short	Nothing updated and no responses in one year - assuming folded 5/24/21
8/31/2021	Orange Pulp Literary	www.clunkyoranges.com	Lines and Curves	Flash	Website gone, appears to have shut down 9/5/21

Sample of the Other tab of spreadsheet

The final tab on my personal spreadsheet is also for rejections, but instead of being arranged by date, they're arranged by story. This way, I can easily scroll to the story I'm trying to check on and see whether I submitted it to a market already. It's simply for convenience, but I've found it helps me keep track of what stories are still in the submission process, which have sold, and which I've pulled from submitting and published myself first. This is done via color coding. If the entries for the story are red, they're still on submission. If they're gray, I've published them myself. And if they're blue, they've been published by someone other than me. This helps when I'm putting together my collections. If I were submitting reprints, this would tell me which stories to consider. So while it's simply a rearranging for convenience, I do find it quite helpful, and I consult it more than the initial rejection tab.

Date	Submitted To	Website	Title	Type	Date Rejected	Notes
2/25/2021	Nameless Magazine	www.nameless.com	Fever Dance	Form	3/22/2021	
4/7/21	Turtle March Magazine	www.turtle.com	Fever Dance	Personal	5/6/2021	No suspense
9/2/21	Insatiable Appetites	www.hungry.com	Fever Dance	Form	11/5/2021	

Sample of the Rejections tab organized by story instead of date

It is not vital that someone go to these lengths to track their publications. For me, I like having everything organized down to the last detail, but I also enjoy making spreadsheets. This type of spreadsheet is fairly simple, considering it doesn't involve a bunch of mathematical formulas. The important things to track are where stories have been submitted and when, the result, and any necessary contract details. How you do that is up to you. It could be a simple list in a notebook or a folder for emails or whatever else you might be comfortable with. The important thing is to have some way to track your submissions. Remember that this is a job and it's important to keep the details straight as much as possible to deter any foibles or embarrassments.

Now that you've got it submitted and recorded, it's time to set it aside until you get a response and start writing the next thing!

CHAPTER SUMMARY

- There are submission tracking platforms, like Duotrope and Submission Grinder that can be used to keep track of your submissions, rejections, and acceptances.
- You can keep a personal spreadsheet in order to track submissions.
- Some keep track both with a tracking platform and their own spreadsheet.
- The important thing is to keep track so you don't make a mistake and look unprofessional.

CHAPTER 13
REJECTIONS

Rejections can come quick or they can take for-freaking-ever. Either way, rejections are inevitable. The best way to prepare yourself is to acknowledge that there will be more rejections than acceptances, and that those rejections mean you're putting in the foot work and working your business. While it would be dense to say not to get sad or upset about it, what I can do is remind you that they're not judging you, personally, and that stories don't only get rejected because they weren't well written or interesting or even liked by the editor. There are many other reasons for rejections, including that the chosen stories for a publication often need to mesh in discrete ways that the editors know about, but that aren't made known to the world. Meaning your story might be about the Wild West, but all the other stories accepted so far are modern and they're making completely different statements. In other words, rejection does not equal bad.

Whatever the reason, and you will rarely be given one at the beginning of your journey, there are specific steps and rules of thumb to follow when a rejection rolls into ye olde inbox. First of all, don't respond to the rejection. Not to say thank you and not to say, well, anything-else you. The vast majority of editors prefer not to have yet another email to stuff up their inbox, and that includes a thank you for a rejection. Personally, I keep an email folder for rejections, and once I've documented the rejection on my spreadsheet and Duotrope, that email goes straight into that folder. Once upon a time, I would go back through the rejections and print up all the ones I'd gotten on a story before getting that final acceptance. I'd then slide those rejection emails in behind the acceptance email and contract. It brought me some sort of weird satisfaction, but don't ask me to explain how. Eventually, it ceased to become something that was worth my time, so now it's a simple move of an email into a folder, then a dusting of the hands.

Another piece of advice here is to never go online and slam the editor or publication. Don't post on your social media that they're stupid or they suck or they don't have any taste in stories. (Again, don't send that in an email in response to a rejection, either. No-no.) Here's the thing: as vast as the publishing industry is, it's also tight-knit in a lot of ways. Blasting a specific publication, editor, or other person associated with a publisher could easily get back to them. Chances are it wouldn't, but here's the other thing: it may not be that editor seeing your behavior, but it could still bite you in the rear. You see, another publisher or editor, or even another author, could see your behavior and decide not to work with you in the future. This could hurt you in the long run, even if you have no idea of the association. And honestly, while there will always be people who "like" that post or egg you on, there will be just as many people who say nothing, but note the attitude. It's simply more professional to take the rejection and move on without saying anything. The goal should be not to harm the writing community at all.

Not to say that you should never post about a rejection. It's perfectly okay to post you received one and it has you down. That's a good way to get support and let your friends and family help you through an emotional slump. There's just no reason to call out anyone specific over it, whether it's the editor or the publication. Commiseration is one thing; smack talk is entirely another.

TYPES OF REJECTIONS

There are two general types of rejection: personal and form. A form rejection is just that, a copied and pasted rejection that goes out the same way to everyone who gets a rejection. This is the standard and is not intended to be hurtful or distant, but simply intended to get the job done and let you know of your status so you can move forward with submitting elsewhere. The busier magazines get hundreds of submissions each day. There is absolutely no way they can send a personal note with feedback to every single one of those people. Neil Clarke is prolific at *Clarkesworld* for getting rejections out fast. They might come hours after the story is submitted. He has dedicated himself to being quick and responsive, and he makes it happen. There are other's who are equally fast or nearly there, and that's actually pretty considerate if you think about it. You aren't left wondering for months at a time if that story's selling, and you can submit it elsewhere and give it its next chance at life.

The second type of rejection is the personal rejection. These ones are rarer, but they're a boon when you get one. A personal rejection may be as simple as letting you know the story was well written, but simply didn't fit the publication or it can be actual feedback that tells you exactly why the story wasn't chosen. These are valuable, but can still sting, so be prepared for that. If you have to give it a day or two to let the sting wear off before you go back to consider advice given, that's perfectly reasonable. But I do recommend going back at some point and looking over what they said in the personal feedback. I am absolutely not saying to accept every inch of feedback given in a personal rejection and immediately change your story to suit what they've asked for. Don't put that on me, Ricky Bobby. What I'm saying is that it's a good idea to consider it and then see if you agree with it when you re-read your story. You might and you might not.

Personal rejections can also be helpful in identifying where the editor might have misunderstood your story. If they did so in a significant way, you might need a rewrite based off that, not any actual recommendations. I had one editor absolutely decide that the chitinous, killer creatures in my story were giant ants. Nowhere did I state they were giant ants. They were not intended as giant ants. And they didn't match the description of any ant I'd ever seen in my life. Still, the editor multiple times said they wanted to know why the ants had gotten so big, and why did the ants do this thing since it made no sense for ants. That one I had to set down and return to, but when I did, it wasn't to take the writing advice in there since it was mis-aimed, but to consider how I'd described the creatures and make sure they weren't coming across as ants anymore. Annoying, but helpful.

A caution on taking advice you might not agree with on a story: just because one editor felt this way about the story, doesn't mean the next one will. I had one poor little story that first got rejected because a dog was injured, but not killed. The injuring of the dog served a purpose, which was to show how far a character had fallen, that they would harm their dog out of desperation. The dog was fine; the other owner whisked it away and got it help, then put it in someone else's charge while they went back to deal with their partner. My very first rejection on the story stated, "I wish you'd been brave enough to go all the way and kill the dog."

Okay, I thought. *I'll kill the damn dog then.* So I did, and I submitted it to the next magazine. I bet you can guess what their response was, but I'll tell you anyway: "Harming an animal in fiction is never okay. I wouldn't even consider this story because you killed the dog."

I wrote three versions of the story and tested them different places (bear in mind some places say in their submission guidelines that no harm may come to animals or the story will not be considered, and I, of course, follow those guidelines and do not submit stories of the harm variety to them). No matter what, I could not get the right version in front of the right person when it was between the dog getting harmed and the dog getting killed. So in that third version I completely removed the dog, which broke my heart because I actually loved that dog and it was a real character in the story to me. RIP, Chauncey. And instead of submitting it again, I waited until I put together my first solo collection and I slapped that dog-free story into my collection as one of a couple never before published stories I'd included. Because I couldn't even decide which version to put in my own collection. I'd let the feedback burrow too deep into my head, and I doubted every decision I made. If you're curious, the person with the issue killed a person instead. Something had to happen to show the enormity of the problem.

Getting back to personal rejections, the no-response rule can be tricky. The well-trained polite person inside me wants to thank them for taking the time to send me personal feedback. It took extra effort, after all! But I have purposely asked various slush readers and editors if I should respond with a thank you to those at least, and the answer has been a resounding "no." Still, I sometimes have to sit on it and convince myself not to send that thank you email. You may choose differently, and that's your choice.

CRICKETS (NO RESPONSE)

Actually, there's a third type of rejection: none. There are markets who post on their website that a story should be considered rejected after x days. While there's a part of me who finds that kind of rude, at least they let you know. There's probably a perfectly good reason for that rule, most likely having to do with the amount of time editors have to dedicate to what is usually a volunteer position on top of day jobs. Sigh, and stick that puppy in your rejections. However, there are also markets that don't say that, but they also never send a rejection. I've had my share of publishers who had to get a book to market quickly, so I only found out my story hadn't made it in when the published book popped up in my feed because I knew people who were in it. I'm not going to lie, that felt like a huge slap in the face. It hurt. I felt it in my gut. They couldn't even be bothered to send a rejection or let people know, and it sucked. Again, I imagine it came down to limited time and unlimited submissions, but it's still a tricky thing to deal with, and there will be surprises sometimes, especially if you're submitting a lot of stories.

Before you consider a story rejected, send a quick query to the editor to follow up on your submission. This is another thing you'll want to scour the submission guidelines page for, because some publications have an email address dedicated solely to queries. It's typically as simple as query@thenameofthepublication.com, but check their page to be sure. Sometimes they want the query sent to the same email the submission went to. Always check. There are also many markets who will specifically request that no queries be made until a certain period of time has passed, so be sure to honor that, as well. They have a better idea of their response times, and know about how long it takes them to get back to you. They base the query time on that. This is actually a place where using a submission program helps, because you can check the most recent responses in Duotrope and Submission Grinder and see if there are any patterns and if you should assume it's rejected, query, or keep waiting. You can also reach out to fellow writers who've been published by that publication to see how long it took them to hear back.

The query should be very basic. I typically find my initial email (if that's how it was submitted) and forward it with a short query that looks like this:

"I'm following up on my submission of Kinky Housewives on October 25 to find out the status. Thank you for your time."

You can write it however you like, but it should be polite, brief, and succinct, and it should list the story title and when it was submitted. This, plus having your email address and the original subject line, will allow them to look in their emails and respond. Or not. Some won't respond even to the query. For me, that typically means I'm not interested in submitting to them again, and I go ahead and assume the story was rejected. Then I move on. You can choose how long you'll wait for a query response, and then scrap it when you haven't heard back by then. I usually give it a couple weeks, and I check to see if they're actively working (as in, does Duotrope show that people are reporting receiving rejections and acceptances during this period). If they're sending responses, but have ignored my email, it's assured I won't hear back.

FINAL THOUGHTS ON REJECTIONS

Every publisher does things different. You'll get a feel for the ones you interact with the most, even if all those interactions are rejections, which your dream markets assuredly will be at some point. I want to reiterate here that you shouldn't beat yourself up about rejections, nor should you give yourself a hard time for being sad about rejections. Sometimes you may even be angry about them. As long as that stays with you, that's okay and even normal. Give yourself a mourning period, preferably no more than a day or two, then smack that baby on the butt and send it back out. That's a weird way to put it, huh? What I mean is, if you decide to edit it before resending, get on that, then send it back out when you're done. If you like it just the way it is, send it out to a different market as soon as you're ready. The secret is to always be ready to turn that story around and submit to the next place, because someone, somewhere, is going to like your story. Given, there will be stories that never sell. They may waste away in a folder for months and years. Maybe they're meant to, but maybe you think that story is really good. We'll talk about some other options for it in Part V. For now, watch for openings that might fit the story, and send it out when you see those.

A final note before we close this chapter: do not ever resubmit the same story to the same market unless they've asked you to resubmit after a rewrite. If they have outright rejected it, that's it. Most publishers have a record of the stories and writers they've rejected. Probably those emails are stored somewhere, and they could even pull up that original version if they wanted to put that much effort in, which they probably don't. it's bad form, and above all, we're trying to be professional writers here and be taken seriously. Once you've gotten a rejection on a story from that market, that's it for that story with them. They don't want to read it again.

Once again, keep sending stories. Keep turning them around when they're rejected. Keep working your business. Do what you want with the rejections, whether you save them in some way, possibly to wall-paper a room, or you delete them instantly and never think about them again. If you need to, seek support from friends and family or go read about how many times such and such famous author got rejected before they finally hit it big. Whatever works for you here. The important thing is to persist and not let rejection get you down. I like to aim for a certain number of rejections each year. Thus, they've become part of my goal. I don't send them to publications they wouldn't fit so I can hit that goal, but I know that I get a certain percentage of acceptances as compared to rejections, and that means that the more rejections I get, the more acceptances I'll get, too. That's what my spreadsheet's for.

CHAPTER SUMMARY

- Rejections can be form, personal, or nonexistent.
- Form rejections are the standard and what you'll likely see the most of at the beginning of your career.
- Personal rejections can give useful feedback or feedback that lets the writer know some tweaking may be necessary.
- Do not assume that all feedback must be assimilated into your story.
- Don't post tirades against an editor or publication if you get a rejection.
- Don't respond to rejections.
- Do feel free to post on your personal social media that you're sad you got a rejection. Commiseration can be nice.
- If you never hear back, query the publisher. If you still don't hear back, assume it's a rejection.
- It's inevitable that you'll be sad about at least some of your rejections, but don't beat yourself up or consider yourself a failure.
- Go for no. Collect those rejections. It means you're working.
- Do not rewrite and resubmit unless you have been specifically asked to.
- Keep writing. Keep submitting. Keep going!

CHAPTER 14
REWRITE REQUESTS

There's a weird limbo between acceptance and rejection, and that limbo is called the rewrite request. In the entirety of my short story career so far, I have received only two of these. One of them dealt with the ant example I gave in the last chapter, and while I did do a portion of the rewrites requested, I did not honor the ones involving making the creatures more ant-like. Because they weren't bloody ants. So I did my own edits to make clear they weren't ants, and I still got rejected in the end. The other rewrite ended in an acceptance. The point in this is to make it clear that a rewrite request is not going to be an automatic acceptance, even if you honor exactly what they've told you they'd like to see, so don't make assumptions about it. Once you send the modifications, you're waiting once again for that acceptance or rejection.

It needs to be clear that you are free to turn down the request and take the rejection. Just let them know with a simple "thank you, but I would prefer not to make changes at this time" or whatever you're comfortable with as a response. As long as it's polite. Again, we're trying not to burn bridges here, because there is not an inexhaustible list of places to submit. While I'll remove markets that don't work for me, usually because of how they treat submitters, I'd prefer not to get the boot from their end. In short, you can't fire me, I quit.

Should you decide to do the rewrite, it is up to you how much credence you give to any suggestions they've given you. After all, this is *your* artistic vision, not someone else's. Your visions for a particular story might not meet theirs. That doesn't mean another editor won't like it just the way it is. When doing a rewrite, carefully consider which changes you'll make and get that work done within whatever deadline they've given you to turn around the rewrite. Most will give a deadline, but some won't. If they don't, it is a good idea to respond that you'd like to rewrite it, but would like guidance on the preferred turn around time. If you're not comfortable querying that, set a reasonable goal, like one week, and get it back in that time. Don't send it two months later and think they're going to care about it anymore. They've since read two million other stories and forgotten the rewrite they requested.

Got other changes you want to make, and it drove you nuts after you submitted it? This may not be the time, but that's up to you. They *will* notice other changes if they're substantial, and they might wonder why you chose to do that. Maybe that part was one they liked. If you really feel your story is stronger for those other changes, it's your decision whether to make them during the rewrite or wait to see if you get accepted or rejected. If you get a rejection, then you've got the perfect opportunity to improve your story before sending it off to the next market. If you get the acceptance, well, it gets tricky here. If you decide you want that change put in anyway, you may then lose that sale. If you're more interested in the publication than the change, you'd be best served to keep it as is since that's how they accepted it.

Though rewrite requests are pure limbo, and make no guarantee of an acceptance after the rewrite, they should be seen as a promising response, anyway. It means this editor liked aspects of your story and writing enough that instead of outright rejecting the material, they've asked for some changes that they feel will make it better and, hopefully, publishable. That means they see promise. Whether the rewrite ultimately ends with an acceptance, someone liked your story. And if you're curious, that not-a-bloody-ant story sold as it was to the very next market I submitted it to. They got it. But I at least had a new experience with the publisher who rejected it, and every learning experience is a gain in this career.

CHAPTER SUMMARY

- You may get a rewrite request instead of an outright rejection or acceptance.
- It is up to you whether you take them up on the request to rewrite it. If you do, it is not guaranteed to be accepted. If you don't, it's almost guaranteed the story will be rejected unless they say otherwise.
- Only do a rewrite you're comfortable with.

CHAPTER 15
ACCEPTANCES

Here we are at the acceptances, so get your confetti and cheer squad ready. There's more work when you get an acceptance, but it's happy work. It's someone-liked-my-story work. It's good-news work. It's OMG-I'm-going-to-be-published, work. You get the point.

The first thing to do when you've gotten the acceptance (after you've stopped dancing around the room, that is) is to review the contract terms they've sent you. Some acceptance emails will come with an attached contract, while others won't. It may be that they have a contract on their website that they've expected you to look at before submitting (in which case, it would be clearly referenced in the submission guidelines) or that they will send the contract later, which they'll typically mention in the acceptance email. The ones that intend to send it later are usually holding the contract until you accept your acceptance, basically. Meaning after you write back a response that indicates you're happy to publish with them and/or the story is still available (depending upon what they asked for in their initial email), they'll respond with the contract. The ones who do this are often the ones that allow for simultaneous submissions to other markets at the same time. For all they know, you've sold it elsewhere, but failed to tell them (not a great thing to do.)

Look the contract over thoroughly. If there's something that doesn't make sense or that rubs you in the wrong way, consult an attorney or at the very least a published friend who has experience with contracts. This is a legally binding contract, and not something to enter into lightly. Make sure you're comfortable with it. This includes the ones listed on the website, which you should have already been comfortable with or you shouldn't have submitted in the first place. The ones on the website sometimes have verbiage indicating that you accept the terms of the contract by submitting the story.

As far as what to look for, here is some general guidance:

- Who holds what rights and for how long?
- How and where will it be published?
- Make sure they've gotten the title ("The Work") and your name ("The Author") correct, as well as any other identifying information for you or them ("The Publisher"), including the publication in which your work is to appear.
- Do you agree with the payment amount?
- How and when will they be paying you (usually upon signed contract, upon publication, or within x days of publication)?
- The stipulated publication time period and if rights revert if it isn't published within a certain period. Ensure you feel the time period is reasonable.
- There may be a section on the type and amount of editing allowed, and whether the author will be consulted to okay the edits.

In short, make sure you read the entire thing and understand what you're signing. If you aren't clear on the details, do your research, check with an attorney, or request clarification from the publisher. There are some great resources online, often through professional writer's groups or guilds, that provide general information on contracts.

If you don't agree with the contract terms, you can try writing in your accepted terms and returning the contract. If they don't agree with your changes, they'll turn them down. If you aren't happy with the final terms, you should turn down the contract, and thus the publication of your story with them. That can be hard to do, personally, but it's best to be comfortable with any contract you're signing and to turn down those you don't agree with.

Once you're happy that the contract makes sense and the terms are agreeable, sign and return the contract. Some publishers offer digital signatures, some will ask for your name to simply be typed in, but most will ask for the contract to be printed and signed, then scanned, and the scan of the contract emailed back to them. The publisher should counter-sign, if they did not do this before sending the contract to you, and send a copy of that final, doubly signed contract. You can request it if they don't. Bear in mind that publications typically have a quick turn-around time, which means they can only wait so long to get the contract back from you. Be sure to do whatever you need to within a reasonable time. I aim for 24 to 48 hours.

This isn't the end of your work upon acceptance. There may be further communications, including a proofreading and/or edits. Most publishers will seek authorization on any major edits, though they may have provided in the contract that minor edits don't need authorization. They will send the edits in a document that allows you to accept or deny them, typically in Google Docs or via a Word attachment. Always bear in mind that you do not have to okay all their proposed edits, but be clear on what the contract said about edits when you go into it, because what you signed is binding. If you feel the edits are detracting from the story as you intended it, or you simply don't agree with them, turn them down. Understand that it could mean the story won't be published, but chances are that they would not have offered a contract if there was a significant change required, unless they'd mentioned that change in the initial correspondence. That would have involved an actual rewrite request before offer of publication. Nobody on either side of the publishing contract wants to put in unnecessary work on something only to have it not published in the end. For the most part, edits you get will be for typos, grammar, and clarity.

Edits are not always sent. In fact, more publications take the story as is than require extensive edits. Some will send a PDF with the semi-final book in it and ask you to proofread for issues in your story and/or let them know if there are any edits you need. Just as with the rest mentioned above, ensure you honor any requested turnaround time on edits and proofreading. Maintaining a good relationship with publishers is important, and respecting their time is a good way to do that. Plus, if they have a publication date and you don't return requested items by that time, they will have no choice but to remove your story from the publication in order to get it to press on time. Magazines tend to have tighter schedules than anthologies, especially those who publish monthly.

Once everything is turned in, it's a matter of waiting again. The publisher may give a definite publication date or they may give a window of time. It's a good idea to keep an eye on the publication website, because they don't always notify their authors when the publication has been released. I've had a few surprises, so I always check in regularly via the website or social media until the publication comes out. In addition, this means you should be monitoring your expected payment. If the payment was due to you upon publication, it should be paid to you within a few days of publication. Don't hesitate to contact the publisher if the publication or payment do not come by the contracted time. If this happens, it's time to send a polite query. Sometimes publication gets pushed back or they're simply behind. If that's the case, they'll let you know. Also, check the website and social media to make sure they're still in business, as publications close regularly, and many don't contact the pending authors to let them know, though some do.

If there is no information stating a publication has closed and you don't hear back on the polite query, your next steps are entirely up to you. You may try to query again, perhaps less politely. Whether involving an attorney is worth it is up to you. It may also be possible to track down other authors to see if they know what's going on. Oddly, being in the short story world occasionally involves some detective work to track things down. Sometimes an answer is all you're going to have, and you can start to recirculate the story if the magazine has gone under. If the story gets published but you don't get paid, they've breached your contract. Make of that what you will, as I'm not an attorney.

Something else that may happen is that you don't get a contract, but your story gets published and you get paid (or not). I've had two publications never send a contract and not have one on their website. Both these publications paid what they owed me, so I took it in stride. I'd gotten an acceptance email and agreed to give them my story in writing. They paid what their website said they paid. There was nothing for me to contest in these cases. Had they published it, but then not paid me for the story, I would have had to pursue legal avenues. Most likely, I would have contacted them over the dust up to see if they would take care of it (as in, pay me for my story) before making it a legal matter.

In a third case, I got an acceptance, didn't get a contract, but was told the expected publication date. When that date rolled around, I contacted the editor and inquired as to why it hadn't been published. I was given a reason and a new date of publication. This happened twice more. I finally withdrew the story and submitted it elsewhere. I note these cases so you're aware that not everything goes perfectly every time. Strange things can happen. Treat them as learning experiences and do the best you can to resolve them. This is also why I'm thorough about keeping an eye on expected publications. They don't always notify you when they'll come out, and they don't always send a contract, though they should do the latter. There's nothing quite like the surprise of finding out your story's been published in a book or magazine and you had no idea it was out there.

But let's return to better things. The story comes out on time and you get paid. This is how the vast majority of your interactions will go. Now there's an unspoken agreement that you'll help promote the publication you're in. That means sharing it on your social media and website, and in general boosting the signal about it. For me, the marketing starts once I've signed the contract. At that time, I post on my social media and website that I've sold a story and when it will come out in the publication. If I don't have the date of publication, I make that a second post once I have the information. This gets the excitement started for those who will want to buy it. I then post upon release. I will go more into marketing in Part VI. There, we'll also cover getting cheaper copies via the publisher, and what you can do with those. The short version is that you can sell these at the cover price and make a bit of money if you do it right. Publishers will have provided information on whether they provide contributor copies and wholesale pricing in the contract.

Make sure you're keeping track of your publications. Previously mentioned spreadsheets and programs will help with this. Here, you should keep track of expected publication dates, payments and payment dates, and the date you can be expected to get your rights back. This will make it easier to know if the publication or payment date have passed, and you'll know when to take action if and when they don't. This is also a good place to keep track of buy links and other pertinent information and links so you have it all in the same place. All of this may come in handy later.

CHAPTER SUMMARY

- First thing you do upon getting an offer of publication (acceptance) is to read the contract and make sure you agree to the terms set forth.
- Try to go over the contract and return it in a timely manner.
- If you don't agree with the terms, do not sign. You can handwrite changes and return to the editor to see if they agree.
- After acceptance, you may get edit requests. Turn these around by the deadline given or as quickly as possible.
- Always help promote a publication you're in; it's an unspoken contract and expectation.

CHAPTER 16
OTHER POSSIBLE OUTCOMES

Not every submission will get a response. Programs like Duotrope and Submission Grinder will also show average response times and current responses (within the last thirty days), which, in addition to the query period mentioned on the publication's website, will tell you how long you should wait before querying the publication. How long you wait, beyond the requested query period, is up to you. You might be patient and give it some extra time, but ultimately there comes a point where they're wasting your time and keeping you from submitting that story elsewhere where it might find a home. I can say that I typically give it more time than the publication asks for, but I will ultimately query if, say, my story is at the maximum time reported for pieces currently out. If they're considering the story, this might give them a kick in the butt to accept it. It could also be the kick that tells them to reject it. There's no way to know how that will shake out, but either way it's not selling if it's in limbo.

If there's no response to a query, the next step is to withdraw the submission. This can be done with a brief, polite email to the publication letting them know that you are withdrawing the story from them. You don't have to tell them why. Simply state, "I am withdrawing X from consideration." If they have both a submission email and a query email, you can send the withdrawal to either one. However, if you didn't hear back on a query, it might be best to send that withdrawal to the submission email instead, simply because they may not be monitoring that query email as well as the submission email. You likely won't hear back from them, so don't have any expectations that you will. You've done your due diligence by withdrawing the story, and you're free to submit it elsewhere.

This may also be necessary if you've done simultaneous submissions and sell the story to another market. You're not required to give a reason for the withdrawal, but if they allow simultaneous submissions, it shouldn't hurt to let them know the withdrawal is because of a sale. That will be your choice to make. It's bad business to not withdraw the story if you've sold it elsewhere, but what you do beyond that is up to you. I've actually gotten very nice congratulations and a request to send something else when I've been honest about withdrawing due to a sale to another market. This was, of course, when both markets were open to simultaneous submissions.

If a publication has gone under, it probably goes without saying that there's no need to send a withdrawal letter. The business is closed. If you had a contract with them, it's null and void now, so you can simply treat the story as if it were free and clear and send it out on submission elsewhere. I do recommend documenting it so you have a record of what happened. On my personal spreadsheet, this and any withdrawals go on the "Other" page, so they don't count as rejections. There are also options on Duotrope for publications that didn't respond or for stories that have been withdrawn. Either way, make a note and get that story back out there.

CHAPTER SUMMARY

- You may get no answer after sending a submission.
- If there has been a significant passage of time, send a query asking about your submission. Be sure to check their submission guidelines to see how long they ask you to wait before querying.
- If you get no response on the query, send a withdrawal email.
- The publication may have gone out of business. This may be researchable by looking at their website, social media, or searching online. If they're out of business, no need to withdraw. Just submit your story elsewhere.
- Make note of any withdrawals, queries, and stories pulled for no response.

PART FIVE
OPTIONS

What to Expect:

- Submitting reprints
- Self-publishing single stories
- Book covers
- Back cover copy / Story description
- Publishing collections
- Query letters
- Purchasing ISBNs
- Self-publishing platforms

CHAPTER 17
SUBMITTING REPRINTS

One of the wonderful things about short stories is that they're not dead in the water once you sell them. There are several options for next steps when it comes to short stories for which you've regained the rights. Any sale, if it's legitimate, has an end period where the rights revert back to the author, which means the author gets to decide what to do with it next. While most people probably just let it lapse into oblivion, there's no reason why you shouldn't be using those stories to make a little more money. Squeeze the last bits of juice out of them if you want to.

One way to do this is to submit them as reprints to markets that accept reprints. Many don't, but plenty still do. Reprints are submitted the same way unpublished stories are, for the most part. They need to be formatted the way the publication's submission guidelines require, and their guidelines will also state whether there are any special instructions. Just be sure to include the original publication name and year of publication. Never turn in a story that has been previously published without giving proper reference and stating it's a reprint.

Examples of small changes a publication may want for a reprint submission are things as minor as putting "REPRINT" in the subject line or sending it to a separate submission email. Duotrope and Submission Grinder have a box that can be checked so any search will require the publication to be open to reprints. If the publication states they don't take reprints or don't mention them at all, don't submit the already published story to them. This one's pretty simple. Though if you really want the publication to reprint your story and they don't say whether or not they take reprints, it's safe to query. Just be sure you've thoroughly checked their website to ensure they haven't mentioned it.

In addition, you need to make sure any contract you sign for a reprint states that you are giving them "Reprint Rights," "Second Serial Rights," or something along those lines. If it says you're giving any sort of "First Rights," the contract is not correct, and you need to get the right one. Signing a paper saying you're giving them rights you absolutely can't be giving them can come back on you legally.

Also important to note is that there are publications that solely want audio rights to a story, so if the story is sold to one publisher who does not take any audio rights, that story can be immediately submitted to an audio-only publication, such as a podcast. There should be no waiting period on that, but make sure you've read both the contract on the non-audio sale and the submission guidelines on the audio-only site before submitting, and be sure to include any information they ask for. You can be honest and say that the story has been sold to a print publication that doesn't take audio rights. For all any of us know, that may increase the chances of it being picked up by the audio-only market. Like I said, squeeze all the juice out.

Here's the other thing about reprints. You can sell that same story to as many markets as you desire, as long as you observe all your contractual obligations and are honest about where it's been published before. If you're reselling the same story repeatedly, you typically just have to reference the first place it was published, but pay attention to whether they ask for more information than that.

To be clear, reprints aren't going to net a ton of money. Not usually, anyway. Reprint payments are less than payments for original works. However, every five dollars adds up over time, especially if your focus is on short stories. It also means more exposure for that story and for you as an author. This isn't going to make you a millionaire any more than selling the original stories will. But every publication is a notch on your belt.

CHAPTER SUMMARY

- Once rights have been returned to you, you can submit that same story as a reprint to markets who publish reprints.
- Make sure your reprint contract reflects that these are "Reprint Rights" or "Second Serial Rights."
- Always give correct attribution to the first place that published the story.
- Always be clear that the story is a reprint when submitting.
- If you did not give rights for a specific format, such as audio, to the first publisher, you still have the first rights to give the audio format to a publisher.
- You can sell a reprint as many times as you want.

CHAPTER 18
SELF-PUBLISHING INDIVIDUAL SHORT STORIES

Another option for reusing short stories once your rights have reverted is to upload them individually to Amazon. You can, of course, also do this with unsubmitted/unpublished stories if you want to go this route first. This book isn't about self-publishing, which is a topic unto itself, so I won't go into proper formatting and such, but it's easy to find instructions via Amazon for how they expect a manuscript to be formatted. In addition, there are tons of resources online that will walk you through the best font choices, the best types of covers, book sizes, and more. Whatever you put out yourself needs to look professional, and that means doing your homework. The largest chunk of work will be at the beginning, that first run-through, but each time after you self-publish something it will get easier and easier to format it to their specifications and put the stories up.

Typically, solo short stories are put up for $.99 to $2.99. There's a delicate balance between pricing to make money and pricing to make sales. Most short stories will be at $.99. It's very important to be clear in the description and even in the title that this is a single short story. Disgruntled readers have no issue leaving nasty reviews if they buy what they think is an entire book and find out it's a 5,000-word short story. One way to make this clear is to put it in the title. Example: *Munchkins in Space: A Short Story*. It's simple and straight forward, and it ensures that anyone reading a review of someone upset that it was a short story will scoff, because they can clearly see in the title it's a short story. Therefore, it's the reviewer who's a jerk, not the author.

BOOK COVERS

Putting up a short story isn't as simple as formatting it and slapping it up there. It's important to have an attractive cover. Yes, even a single story requires a cover. If this is something you're excellent at or have a resource for, great, but most people have to pay for a book/story cover. Cover artists can be found on websites like Fiverr, Deviant Art, 99 Designs, and 100 Covers. There are many more, so have fun looking around. In self-publishing it can be helpful to go in with some ideas of what you want. Do searches in your genre to see what the covers look like, which ones are selling the best, and what sticks out to you on the covers. Knowing what catches your eye will tell you what should be included on your own book cover. I like to also put together a list of "visuals" from my stories to give to the artist at the beginning. It's how I ended up with a creepy outhouse on the cover of one of my books. It worked, though, as that was the most asked about story within the book. If there's a main character that might be featured on the cover, give a basic description so your Native American main character doesn't end up as a redhead on the cover (unless, of course, your Native American character does, in fact, have red hair).

Be prepared to share what you're looking for in the cover, if there are any colors you want featured, what visuals you're seeking, and be prepared to give them comparables from the ones you looked up, so the artist knows what they're working with. If you go with an artist on Deviant Art, they may need more guidance, as they might not know covers as well as someone on a site dedicated to book design. An experienced book cover designer will know how to draw the eye to the right places at the right time, what colors stand out, and what a book cover should look like, in general. The more experience they have, the more they may cost. Here, it's important to weigh how many sales you might realistically get on a single short story versus a longer book, and therefore what your cover design budget is. Chances are slim that you'll make $1000 off a short story on Amazon. A $50 book cover might be more realistic. The short story may also end up losing money. It's a good idea to do this once to give it a try, especially if you're willing to do the footwork to do it right in the first place, but also to research and troubleshoot what may be going wrong and right once it's published.

FRONT MATTER

Make sure you get proper attributions from the cover artist. You will need to know the name, date, and copyright for any images they used. You will also need to know what name the artist would like in the attribution. They might prefer their business name be cited over their actual name. This information will need to be documented with the published story, typically in the front matter. Front matter is the initial information that precedes the actual story, such as a title page and a copyright page, which would also include your ISBN. Leaving off proper attribution can lead to accusations of theft and bring on legal issues. Plus, you want to ensure the cover artist and the creators of any images are given due credit, just as you would expect due credit for your written work.

STORY DESCRIPTION

Something else you'll need is a description. Basically, you need a description of the story that will intrigue the reader and make them want to spend their money to buy this particular short story. A synopsis. Keep it short—only a few sentences—and make it interesting. Don't give away spoilers or endings. Make it fast paced and create questions if you can. Writing something that makes the reader want to know more is the only way to pull them in after they click the link because the title and cover brought them in. Basically, if you understand the sales funnel, the cover is the top of the funnel. It's the first thing the reader will see, and it's designed to catch them and make them click to find out more. That story description and price are going to be the bottom of the funnel. They are the things that will help the reader make that final decision. Buy or not buy? If it sounds interesting and the price is right, they're in. You've just sold a story to a reader. This one's especially important to run by friends. Send it to a few of them (with their permission—no one likes to be used without agreeing to it first) and ask what they think. Does it make them want to read more? Would they buy it based on the description? Would they change anything about it? Is there anything that turns them off?

OTHER CONSIDERATIONS

With a single short story, chances are you will only be doing an e-book. Putting out a hard copy of a single short story is pushing your luck. There is the possibility of doing a chapbook-type setup, too, but that would involve research outside of this book. A chapbook is a short paper publication, up to about forty pages. They're usually inexpensively bound. Some small publishers put out chapbooks as part of their business plan, so it would be worth checking these publishers out to see what their chapbooks look like and whether they have a source you can go through for the same sort of thing. For chapbooks, you'd have to use something other than Amazon, most likely.

Short story e-books are a good thing to put exclusive on Amazon so they can be on Kindle Unlimited, which allows readers to pay a single fee for the month and read anything marked as KU for the rest of the month. To do this, authors must make their book exclusive under the Kindle Select option, which also allows the author to do special offers and discounts once per term. Authors with KU books are then paid a portion of the amount paid for KU subscriptions, depending upon page reads their stories got. It can also lead to more exposure for your writing, and may bring readers to other publications you might have out, whether those are books or other short stories. Be sure to research KU/KS and understand the contractual obligations you'll have. For a short story, it's a great way to go. However, it means you will not be allowed to put that e-book out anywhere else during your contracted time with them. You can't put it free on your website and upload it to any other platforms. Be clear on this and other requirements before you dive in. With short stories, there aren't a bunch of platforms running against Amazon, which is why I specifically address them in this chapter. It is possible to publish a short story on Smashwords, but it may not lead to any sales at all. This is something you'll have to weigh against the benefits of enrolling in KU.

However you decide to distribute your individual short story, this is a nice way to bring in a little extra money. Whether it's a reprint or you went straight to e-publishing with it, it may help you gain new readers and sell other stories you have out. Just as with selling reprints to other markets, this isn't intended as a get-rich-quick scheme. But each small piece of income you set up will eventually add up.

CHAPTER SUMMARY

- Short stories can be uploaded individually to Amazon.
- Pricing is typically $.99 to $2.99 for a short story.
- Be sure to list in the title and/or description that this is a short story.
- A book cover is a necessity, even with a short story.
- Professional-looking book covers can be attained from art and book cover websites for relatively low cost.
- Give proper attribution to all artists involved with your cover.
- You will a story description to draw readers in and tell them what it's about.
- Individual short stories will usually be in e-book only.
- Individual short stories are good candidates for Kindle Unlimited.

CHAPTER 19
COLLECTIONS

nother use for short stories is to bundle them together into solo collections of your work. This could be done through a traditional publisher or as a self-published piece. Either way is valid.

TRADITIONAL PUBLISHING

Collections can be a hard sell for traditional publishers if the author isn't otherwise well known. Stephen King, for example, can sell a collection of short stories to the big publishers no problem. The guy that lives down the street from you, maybe not so much. It's worth a try, though, if that is what's important to you. Their bottom line is going to be whether it will sell tens of thousands of copies, and your job is to convince them it will.

If going the traditional route, or at least wanting to try it first, there's another place where a split decision has to be made. Do you want to get an agent or submit directly to smaller publishers? If you want to get an agent, you need to do your research on agents and find ones that will take not only your genre, but also collections of short stories. Many won't list collections in their bios, so it may take extra legwork. One way to find agents who will work with short story collections is to look at already published collections of short stories and check the comments in the back for the agent name. This will also show who the publisher is, so you'll know a publisher to submit to if you want to skip the agent search.

If you're skipping the agent and going straight to a publisher, make sure they take unsolicited manuscripts, in addition to accepting short story collections and the pertinent genre. They can be found the same way as agents. Duotrope can be searched for publishers of short story collections and now for agents, too. In addition, there are sites like Query Tracker (querytracker.net) and Publishers Marketplace (publishersmarketplace.com) that provide a searchable database where you can also keep track of submissions. On Twitter, there's a hashtag for finding agents and publishers interested in specific things: #MSWL. This stands for Manuscript Wish List. Here, agents and editors say what they're seeking and not getting enough of, which can be great if what you're selling fits their needs.

Whether submitting to an agent or a publisher, you've now reached a point where you have to write an actual query. The basics will be similar to a novel query, with an introduction that includes the length, genre, and the fact that it's a short story collection. It's a lot harder to come up with a quick synopsis that describes each short story, so you'll want to pick a few stories whose premises will be good to throw out as lures. It might help to write a quick, interesting, one-line description of each story so you can pick the best ones. If the stories you're bundling have a consistent theme throughout, it's important to mention that, as well. Also, make sure you mention the markets where these stories were published before. These need to be the actual magazines and anthologies, not one you've self-published on Amazon without having been published before unless you can show a report that states you sold extremely well and have a plethora of reviews. Seeing that the stories found a market will enhance the image of the collection.

Just as with a cover letter on a short story submission to a magazine, it's important to research the agent or publisher you're querying and use the correct name. The first paragraph is often an introduction to your collection, which is where you will put the genre, theme, length, and pertinent information of that stripe. If you've actually met the agent or editor, say at a writer's conference, you would also want to mention that in the opening of the letter. In the next paragraph, you might want to go into a couple of the stories, with those quick synopses you worked out. No more than one-to-two lines per story, and don't do all the stories, only the most interesting. Mention any accolades or reviews you've gotten on the individual stories mentioned. In the third paragraph, put your biographical information, such as your experience as a writer, if you belong to any professional writer's groups, and any schooling, major workshop experience, or contests won. This is where you're selling yourself, rather than your stories. They may end up asking for a couple of the stories or for a portion of the manuscript. That's great news! Go from there.

SELF-PUBLISHING

The other option is to self-publish the collection. These stories have been published before, so they've hopefully been professionally edited already. That already makes it less of an expense than a novel that would require paying an editor to look over, though that's still on the table if you think it would be a good idea. Some magazine publishers don't necessarily edit the stories beyond some basics. Personally, I also like to include a few "new to you" stories, ones that have not been previously published. While it's a good idea to have the bulk of the stories be ones you already made some money off of through publishing them in magazines and anthologies, a few bonus reads for your truly dedicated readers who buy your collections in addition to buying each publication you're in (hi, mom) give them something to look forward to and a reason to read the collection instead of just shelving it to support you.

While Amazon is still the primary market for self-published authors, with them holding about 80% of the market share, there are several other options, as well. These include Smashwords, Ingram-Spark, Lulu, Draft 2 Digital, CPI, and others. It's important to research your options before diving in. A combination of these platforms can be used if it's done right. Use extreme caution when considering lesser-known platforms. Some may be vanity publishers, meaning they don't have any real distribution and they will charge a lot of money or have expensive minimums. The best way to research the different platforms is to look for articles and blogs written by successful self-published authors and see who they're using. It's a common topic, which means there's a wealth of information available. Many authors blog about their experiences with the platforms, both good and bad.

One option is to go exclusive with Amazon in the Kindle Select program, which keeps you from being able to release it elsewhere in e-book. (Kindle Select is only for e-books.) The other option is to diversify and release in various platforms. It's a mixed bag, and something you'll need to research and decide on your own. I've tried both releasing it wide with multiple platforms (Amazon and Smashwords, for example), as well as doing the initial release as a Kindle Unlimited deal, meaning it had to be published with *only* Amazon for the contracted Kindle Select term. I find most of my sales are through Amazon, and that I make more money releasing exclusively with Kindle Select first, then also releasing it more widely on Smashwords after removing it from Select (meaning it's still for sale on Amazon, but will not be a free book available to KU readers, and therefore won't earn a piece of the KU pie each month). This is just for collections. Novels and non-fiction might be a different story.

The terms are 90 days for authors, which auto-renews until you go in and remove the book. Once you mark that you want to remove it, the book will remain on KU until that 90-day term is over. Then it's free and clear, and you can put the e-book up elsewhere. I usually keep it in Kindle Select until I start to see the KU page reads lessening. That also allows me to run a couple free or reduced-price specials, one for each term it's enrolled in Kindle Select. That ability goes away once the book is no longer in Select. You can always toggle the price through the dashboard on your own, though, and will just have to do any changes manually.

Smashwords is a great choice to distribute e-books to Kobo, Apple, Barnes & Noble, and other e-book platforms. They don't handle print books at all. They have some deals that can be offered to readers, such as a coupon code that can be used on their site. This is a great way to give something special to newsletter readers. The coupon code goes out in your newsletter, so only your loyal fans get the deal. They also have a big sale twice per year that you can easily enroll your books in, choosing to either make them free, 25% off, 50% off, or 75% off. All you do is click a box to enroll your book, select the discount, then advertise the deals until the sale ends. There are some people who refuse to buy books via Amazon, so going through Smashwords eventually gives those readers a way to get your books. Smashwords is a friendlier platform, because they don't use their power to harm authors who release on multiple platforms, which is something Amazon does. Make sure if you use multiple platforms that you publish direct through Amazon, rather than relying on wide distribution through another platform to do so. That means Amazon usually needs to be the first place you publish it. Otherwise, the other platform will push their distribution to Amazon and you won't be able to put your book up directly through them anymore.

Another major contender is IngramSpark. IngramSpark has a price for putting your book on their site, but it allows bookstores to order directly from the same company they get their traditionally published books from. It also means libraries are more likely to acquire your book, as they'll do so through Ingram. Bookstores and libraries don't go through Amazon or Smashwords. Thus, even if you choose expanded distribution with Amazon, it won't actually get your books on shelves outside the company. There are a lot more technicalities to using IngramSpark, such as whether or not to make your books returnable, which you'd want to research first. When publishing with both IngramSpark and Amazon, it's safest to publish the book with Amazon first, without marking expanded distribution, then use the same ISBN to publish the book with IngramSpark. Ingram has wider distribution, and that distribution includes Amazon. If the ISBN is the same, Amazon will register the push from Ingram, but keep up the version you directly published through Amazon. This is beneficial to you, in that Amazon won't try to block your book. If you don't put your book through Amazon first, they will penalize you once your book comes to them from Ingram. This includes things like delaying shipping, showing your book as out-of-stock, and other issues that will impact your showing in the algorithms. It's a means of competition for them. This is a quick and dirty addressing of the issue, so I reiterate that you'd want to do research before choosing your distribution platforms and the technicalities with each.

Personally, if wanting to use multiple platforms, I'd publish with Amazon first, then through IngramSpark, then add it to Smashwords. Do not use wide distribution on Amazon. Use it with Ingram instead. Ingram distributes to the same e-book companies as Smashwords, so it won't be necessary to do the wide distribution on Smashwords either. But publishing your e-book with Smashwords allows you to use their wonderful discount and sale promotions. It's a great trio if juggled the right way. However, you may prefer to go another way after you do your own research. Whatever you're comfortable with is best. It's you who has to deal with the various hoops. If you want to start simply your first time around, it may behoove you to do only Amazon at first. If you don't go with Kindle Select, you can upload your book to Smashwords whenever you're comfortable, even if it's later on down the line, and skip IngramSpark altogether. The easier the better when you're starting out. Experimenting is better done once you've started to become comfortable with the process.

ISBNS

ISBNs are a vital part of your publishing journey. Note that different publishing platforms may require different ISBNs, as will different formats (e-book compared to print). Make sure to look into the requirements of any publishing platform you're using and adjust accordingly. Many of the platforms will provide you an ISBN upon request, possibly at an extra cost, but it may show them as the publisher instead of you. Also, once used, an ISBN cannot be used on a different book. When making changes to an already published book, a new edition may require a new ISBN. These are all things that will need to be researched depending upon what you're doing and where you're doing it.

It is possible to get an ISBN through Amazon for the print version (they don't require an ISBN on Kindle e-books), but the publisher will then be listed as Amazon. This is not an issue if you're okay with that. My personal preference was to create a publishing house for myself, which also is used for tax purposes, and purchase my own ISBNs directly. This is not what everyone does, and either choice is solid as long as you research it and understand all the ins and outs before deciding what to do. This, again, is outside the purview of this book, but there's a ton of information available online and in book form on self-publishing in order to get more of the specifics. Before entering into this it's important to research the financials, the tax repercussions, and what type of business to set up. Two fabulous books I found to add into my online research for this were *Self-Publisher's Legal Handbook*, by Helen Sedwick, and *Information in a Nutshell: Business Tips and Taxes for Writers*, by Carol Topp, CPA.

It is very important to note that Bowker is the only place you should buy ISBNs. If you simply plug "buy ISBNs" into a search bar, a ton of places will pop up that will be happy to sell you ISBNs. They all get them from Bowker, though, and will likely be marking them up. And that's only for the ones who are reselling legitimate ISBNs. Bowker ISBNs are found at the website www.myidentifiers.com. Don't let yourself be scammed by anyone else. They can be purchased one at a time or in lots. The price per ISBN reduces the larger the lot gets. Note that more people seem to lean toward using the Amazon-provided identifiers for single short stories, but for any sort of book or collection, more use ISBNs they've purchased themselves. I keep a spreadsheet with my purchased ISBNs and where they've been used, plus enter it in my account via Bowker to keep track.

FORMATTING/EDITING/COVER DESIGN

When it comes to formatting, different platforms have different formats they want to see. They're mostly similar, but, for example, Smashwords and IngramSpark have more specific rules than Amazon. This means you can't just do one formatting job and submit it else-where without first checking their formatting requirements. Amazon appears to be the most relaxed on their requirements, so they'll take the formatting from other places, such as Smashwords, without issue.

Figure out which platform you're submitting to has the strictest rules and do those first if you want to be able to submit the same general document everywhere else. Meeting Smashwords' standards means wider reach.

If you're willing to invest the money, there are people who will do all the formatting for a fee. Make sure you do your research into them and ask for references. Contact those references and ask if they were happy with their formatting and whether they had any issues. Look at books given as references. Just as with cover design, the formatting prices will vary widely. The higher the fee, the more experience they typically have. This won't always be the case, so always do your research before paying anyone. Also, ensure they give you a contract. This is true of cover designers, too. There should be a contract. If you're paying someone to edit your collection, there should also be a contract there. Basically, if you're handing your money to anyone else, they should be providing written protection for both of you. That's the sign of a legitimate business exchange.

If you're confident you can do all these things, more power to you. Make sure you do your research on what's required. Amazon will give you a preview before a book goes live, which can be quite helpful. If you have to change any documents to a different format, such as a PDF, ensure you go through and check every single page to review it for issues. Bizarre formatting issues can occur, and it will be problematic for readers, who may return the book or leave a negative review if it looks bad. While it may seem like the actual story should be what carries the book, all the details matter. If someone downloads a book with five words per page because something happened during the upload due to faulty formatting, they're going to be too frustrated to keep reading it. The same goes for a book with a billion typos. Eventually, it becomes too much, and the story isn't worth it.

CONSIDERATIONS FOR BUILDING A COLLECTION

There's more to putting a collection together than throwing a bunch of stories together and publishing them. One thing to consider is how long the collection needs to be. At the very least, it should be over

40,000 words, if possible. While shorter is acceptable, there will be awards it can't be entered for if it's too short. If every 10,000 words make up about 40 pages, 40,000 words will net a 160-page book. That's a nice, reasonable length, and makes the reader feel like it was worthwhile to buy the collection.

Just as with sentence length within a single story, the lengths of the stories need to vary between the covers of the collection. An easy way to toggle this is to make a list with each story and its length and start mixing them up. A super long story should be preceded and followed by a quicker read. It's best not to start the collection with a super long story, though it's not uncommon to end the collection with a longer one. If you have a novella, that might be the place to put it. By the time they reach the ending story, they're fully invested in finishing the collection, so they're more likely to sink their teeth into the long one. I personally prefer putting the longest one a couple stories before the last one, so they get through the big one and have a couple bite-sized stories to finish it off. It also depends upon the strength of your longer story. If it's one of your best pieces, ending with it provides a double bang.

Speaking of which, the collection should open and close with the strongest stories. If this is the longest story, put it at the end. If you're able to ascertain the stronger stories in the collection, they should be scattered throughout at optimal places. Putting the stronger stories at the beginning and end, then putting the second strongest stories about mid-way between the beginning and middle, then the middle and end will help prop up the rest of the collection and keep readers moving through. Your weakest stories shouldn't be in the collection at all, but the weakest of your included stories should be surrounded by good ones. Obviously, different readers will prefer different stories. There's no perfect way to predict how an audience will take a story. The best you can do is use your own judgment on it. I've been surprised by people's choices on what they considered to be standout stories before. Just as there's a person for everyone, there's a story for everyone. It's a matter of finding that right one for the reader.

Bear in mind that, overall, the greatest hook needs to be at the beginning. After that, there must be incentive for readers to continue, which might mean putting more of the better stories in that mix in the first half. As long as you have a couple strong ones for the end and at that three-quarter point, it should draw the reader all the way through if the beginning of the collection has had a solid pay-off.

There may be other considerations within the stories to consider, especially when taking genre into account. For example, because I write horror, if I have a couple horror comedies to include, I'll put those at the end. In doing so, the reader has read the darker stuff earlier, and can end on a slightly lighter note. How light it might be depends upon the stories. This would apply to something that's maybe a slower or more involved read. That one should not be the closer, because it might result in the book being put down without being finished or leave the reader with a bad taste in their mouth if that's how the collection ended. It's just like an individual story or a novel; the reader should leave satisfied. This doesn't mean they leave happy so much as they leave feeling like the collection was worthwhile and they're happy they read it. This aspect of choosing the stories and the order of stories might seem from the outside to not be a big deal, but it turns out it's quite important. Picking the length, tone, and beat of the stories is just like pacing out am individual story, varying the sentence and paragraph lengths, and switching up the beats. It can be powerful or it can be a flop.

Somewhere in the book should be a list of where each story was first published in order to give fair attribution. Include the year, as well. The rest of the date does not have to be included. This list is quick and simple, and is usually best placed at the end of the collection. There's no need to put it at the front or with each story unless that's how you prefer it. A note on front matter, though: because platforms like Amazon allow previewing, there should be as little front matter as reasonably possible. Aside from the necessary copyright page, title pages, and a table of contents, plus any introduction you might want to include to the collection (totally optional), there shouldn't be anything else up front. A dedication can be included up front, but any further notes and thank yous are best left at the end where they won't take up valuable preview space. The idea is to ensure at least part of the first actual story is available to be previewed by the reader. If they can't read any part of the content, that might be a lost sale. Nobody picks up a book at a bookstore and looks at the front matter to determine if the book is for them, so make sure the front matter isn't all they can see in an online preview.

A little something extra you can add, and something that I've gotten a lot of positive feedback on, is a section on what inspired each story or any background on a story. I put this near the end, so people can skip it if they like, but it's there for those who like to hear how a story was birthed. If you can't remember or don't care, no worries. It's not at all an expectation of collections. The reason I put it in is because I really enjoyed reading similar bits in anthologies I'd read, where the editor put an interesting tidbit about the story or author at the beginning or end of each short story. It was a fun addition, and sometimes illuminated things within the story that I might not have noticed on my own.

At the end of the collection, it's a good idea to put a bio and any links to websites, plus a listing of other books by the author. This is your back matter. A big bonus to e-books is that the actual links can be placed in the manuscript, so someone reading on a computer or other link-capable machine can go directly to a link for another book once they've finished the current one and buy it. You've just upsold the reader. This is a great opportunity. I've seen the "other books by this author" section put at the front, but if it's up front they don't know whether they want to buy another book by you yet, and they likely won't want to go all the way back to the beginning to find another book. Instead, close with it. If you can put the beginning of another book by you, whether that's a short story or a chapter, in the back, that might be enough to tantalize them into going for the next one. A big part of providing these short stories in a collection is to make it convenient for fans to find all your stories, but also to lead them to other works by you.

TITLE

Let's close out this chapter by starting at the beginning: titles. Choosing a title for a collection can be tricky, but a good rule of thumb is to use the title of either your best story or the story with the most intriguing title from within the book. If you intend to put out more than one collection over time, tying these together with a theme of sorts can't hurt, either. Two examples of this would be my first two collections: *Blue Sludge Blues & Other Abominations* and *Bruised Souls & Other Torments*. One thing I feel I did wrong in those was to not use the title of an actual story in Bruised Souls. One thing I did right was set that theme of the title along with a phrase that makes it clear this is a dark collection. By putting the portion after the ampersand, I'm trying to show it's a collection of stories, not a single novel. But any way you want to tie things together will work. Having a pattern does help with figuring out titles in the future. Either way, the point is to tantalize and draw in the reader. After a while, they know what it means and what to expect.

IN CLOSING

A helpful website is www.books2read.com. You can enter one of your purchase links on their site and get a universal link to post. This universal link will automatically pull all the places the book is available so that when someone clicks on the link they're taken to a page that shows the different places the book can be bought. The person then clicks their preferred means, such as Kobo, and they're taken there to buy their copy. This works internationally, so if you're publishing in the U.S., but the buyer is in Australia, they'll be taken to the proper site to purchase it in their region. You can use this for any books you're sharing out, even if it's an anthology you're in.

I have purposely avoided giving anything that might be construed as legal advice. That's why I recommended the two business books. Those are written by tax and legal experts, and therefore a much better resource for that end of things. I can say what I've done, to an extent, without saying that's exactly how you should do things. Make sure you do research into self-publishing if you're going in that direction. There are plenty of self-publishing resources to help you in that capacity.

CHAPTER SUMMARY

- Collections can be submitted to agents or editors.
- Query traditional publishers and agents similar to novel queries, but with information on the theme and a couple individual stories.
- Only query agents and editors who take collections.
- Self-publishing is also a valid option for publishing a collection.
- Major self-publishing platforms are Amazon, Smashwords (e-books only), IngramSpark, Draft2Digital, CPI, and Lulu.
- ISBNs are necessary, and can be purchased via Bowker or through submission platforms.
- Formatting, editing, and cover design may require external experts.
- Always include attribution to where any story in your collection was first published.
- Keep front matter brief, where possible.
- Choose your title carefully.

PART SIX
MARKETING

What to Expect:

- Marketing mix – 4 Ps
- Definition of marketing
- Website building/SEO
- Blogging
- Domain name
- Email
- Social media/Scheduling platforms
- Newsletters
- Book outlets & claiming author/book accounts
- Headshots
- Events/Appearances/Appearance kit/Swag

CHAPTER 20
MARKETING INTRODUCTION

Marketing can be the bane of every writer. Most of us like to write, not sell, and it causes a lot of stress and pressure, in addition to taking up a lot of our time. Nobody warned us we'd have to not only be writers, but also businesspeople and salespeople. While writers come from all backgrounds, and therefore there are some salespeople who are also writers, the vast majority of us are not. Still, if we want people to buy our books and give us a try, that means we'll have to do the footwork to make it happen.

One of the most eye-opening things I learned during my time in business school was what marketing actually was. Previously, I had thought of it purely as advertising, but advertising is just a portion of marketing. It's a sub-category. In other words, while marketing does involve selling and advertising, that's not the entirety of it. In fact, marketing starts from the kernel at the center of the idea. As soon as you start writing a story, you've started marketing it. How you write that story is marketing. The words you choose are marketing. The title of the piece is marketing. The length of the piece is marketing. Marketing departments help come up with business concepts and products, which means you were part of that department from the beginning.

The short job description of marketing is ensuring a company and product provide value to the customer. The value is in the story and its presentation. In other words, the value to the customer is the story itself and *you* are the company. People looking for something to read want to find those stories. Your job is to provide them with those stories, meaning you're providing a service. You're giving value to a reader, because readers are your customers, and they want stories! Nobody is forcing stories down someone's throat. Instead, we writers are trying to make a good product and then help people find the very product they're looking for.

Here's a list of the ways you're marketing:

- Writing the story a certain way
- Choosing a catchy title
- Creating characters the reader cares about or identifies with
- Choosing/designing a book cover (when self-publishing a story or collection)
- Packaging the book
- Choosing how to publish the story (submitting to magazines or books, self-publishing)
- Writing a synopsis or back cover copy
- Choosing the price (whether this means the honorarium you accept to sell a story or the price at which you set a self-published title)
- Compiling stories into a collection, and the choices involved with that
- Choosing the platforms where stories/collections will be published
- Elevator pitches
- Attending conferences and conventions and telling others about your story/collection
- How you present yourself as a writer/author
- How you behave on social media/website
- What you post about the book/story on your website/social media
- Conducting interviews about your publications

- Putting lists and links of other publications at the end of a collection
- Linking to your websites/social media
- Networking with other writers, who are typically readers

There are many other ways in which you market yourself and your work, but this is just meant to give you an idea of what marketing actually is. Somehow it takes a bit of the weight off when you look at it from the viewpoint of all of it being marketing, with the actual advertising and selling being a tiny, albeit important, percentage of it. It also helps to understand that you're not trying to be pushy with your product, but are trying to connect with those who are seeking your product. Don't try to force it on anyone. Instead, present yourself and your story/book as interesting, and put out the information that catches people's attention, but also helps them decide if your product is right for them. Then you catch those who are interested and inform those who aren't that maybe this isn't for them. That's completely fair, because no one wants someone reading their work who will ultimately hate it. Honestly packaging and representing your work keeps that from happening and helps find the right readers.

Another way to put this is to simply pass along the American Marketing Association's definition of marketing: "The activity, set of institutions, and processes for creating, communicating, delivering, and exchanging offerings that have value for customers, clients, partners, and society at large." Nowhere in that definition is the need to trick unwilling people into partaking in the product you're selling. While we see plenty of that in hungry salespeople, that's not the true definition of the word, and it should be avoided by making ethical choices in your use of advertising. If you go forward as someone genuinely interested in finding the right readers for your work, you won't have cheated anyone. Your goal should be to leave the buying relationship with both of you happy about the interaction, meaning you're happy you sold a story or book, and they're happy they bought it.

Marketing as a concept involves identifying a need and fulfilling it to the best of your ability. When you think of a story, you've identified the plot, the characters, the genre, and so many other micro-details of the story. That means you've addressed a series of reader needs. If I'm writing horror, I have a marketing segment, or a portion of the reading population, that I'm writing for. I have identified that there is a segment of the population that likes a dark or scary story, and even if I'm not writing to market, I'm writing for that segment. Therefore, I've produced a product that will hopefully fulfill someone else's need, and I will exchange this item of value I've created for something else I value, which would be financial, but also hopefully a positive review. Making someone happy, so to speak, with my story by bringing them some manner of enjoyment is part of my goal, and satisfying that is important. If we didn't care what people thought, we wouldn't put our art babies out there for others to experience, and we wouldn't dread negative reviews. No one likes to be disliked.

MARKETING MIX – 4 PS

There's something called a marketing mix, aka the Four Ps of Market-ing. These are product, price, promotion, and place. This further shows that marketing isn't sitting at a table and asking someone to buy your book.

Product - This is where I reiterate that the product itself is the first part of marketing. We've already discussed this some, but the impor-tant takeaway is that this beautiful creature you've birthed is as instru-mental to the marketing as any other part. Your goal is to create a pleasing and satisfying product that people will enjoy. The product is the bells and whistles, the story, the theme of the story, and whatever you're trying to convey through that story.

Price - This one's pretty simple, but also important. If you choose to sell a short story to a market, you've set a monetary value on that piece. If you choose to sell it for a contributor copy (a free copy from the publisher), that's the price at which you've set the story. This, of course, gets more complicated when it comes to self-publishing a story or a collection, as you are directly setting a price to pass onto the consumer. This is the value you see in the story or book. It's your half of the exchange, meaning it's what you're willing to trade for the creative property you're giving to the reader.

Pricing matters a lot in terms of what will sell. If it's too expensive or the other party doesn't see that the values are equal, meaning they don't think the value of the story matches the value of the cash they're trading for it, they won't purchase it. At the same time, there's a concept that shows pricing something too low actually diminishes the value the customer places on the product. In other words, if you price a short story for $.25 instead of $.99, people may think it's *too* cheap, and therefore that the story itself holds no value to them. It's a complicated line to walk, so this is something that should be researched when self-publishing.

The cost of the product—in this case, the fee due to the platform carrying and selling your product plus the price of any hard copies you purchase to hand-sell—must also be considered when choosing a price. Amazon, for example, changes the percentage you get of the sale price depending upon the price point you set. If the price is too low, they actually take a larger proportion of the sale price than they do for a higher priced product. Their end goal is to get a reasonable share of money out of the sale, so they want authors to price their stories/books in a way that brings in profit. The price also needs to be something that the reader doesn't regret after finishing the piece, which is why it needs to be clear if something is a single short story and why a collection needs to be a reasonable length. In the end, they must be satisfied that what they paid for and how much they paid for it was worthwhile, not a disappointment or letdown.

Promotion – This is the visible marketing aspect. As in, this is where those details we consider sales come into play. Promotion is how the author packages themselves, plus the ways in which the product information are given out. If I choose to attend a conference and take an author table, this is part of my promotion strategy or promotional mix. Posting the story or collection on my social media page is a portion of the promotional mix. Chatting with a person about what I wrote is part of the promotional aspect, as is choosing to pay for an ad. This part of the marketing mix needs to cover whatever ground you're comfortable with and needs to be diversified. Posting only to social media one time and being done just plain won't work. But putting an ad in the paper, being interviewed on a podcast, working a conference author table, sending out a newsletter, swapping posts with another blogger, *and* posting to your social media and website is going to reach more people in more ways, and widen the chances of finding readers who want your story or book. In short, diversifying your promotion across multiple outlets increases your chances of finding readers.

It's also important to analyze the different methods available and to skip those that don't make sense for your particular product. What I mean by this is that I won't attend a children's festival and pay for an author table to sell one of my horror collections (unless, of course, I were to write a collection of short horror stories for pre-teens). Choose the methods that make the most sense for your product, your story. Part of this is also presenting a consistent appearance through all the advertising or promotion, which is a way of branding yourself and your product. This means having a consistent set of messages that are then uniformly put out on all the different formats or channels.

Place – This is how the product gets to the customer. This means choosing the magazine or publication you sell your story to in the first place, but also includes the platforms used to distribute it after the fact. This is choosing whether you will self-publish or look for a publisher for your collection. This also involves whether something is put out in e-book, paperback, audio, or any other form. If you have copies of a book, whether from a traditional publisher or via a self-publishing platform, and you choose to go to local bookstores and consign your book, this is also part of place. Place involves how you get the product to the consumer. Choosing ways you can be proud of falls on you, which also means vetting a magazine before you submit to them. You don't want to sell your story to a publisher who, it turns out, is known for harassing female colleagues at conferences or cheating writers out of royalties. You can't vet this perfectly, as things leak out at different rates, but a quick Google search of a publisher or publication might root out some of these issues if they've started leaking out online.

CONCLUSION

Hopefully, this section has illustrated that marketing is more than we writers typically view it as, and knowing that you were marketing from the moment you came up with a story concept maybe helps make the rest of it easier. For actual marketing tips, I'll be breaking down specific elements of an author's marketing mix and showing some best practices for both marketing a simple short story that's being published by a magazine or anthology and for when you've self-published a short story or collection or put together a collection with a publisher. Marketing a single short story you've had published in a magazine or anthology will be significantly simpler than marketing something you're putting out on your own.

CHAPTER SUMMARY

- You started marketing the moment you decided to write a specific story.
- Marketing is far more than selling a product.
- Marketing includes the creation of the product (your story), the pricing of the product (how much you choose to sell the story for), how you promote it (posting to social media, sending out a newsletter, etc.), and the place (where you make it available, such as the magazine you choose to publish it in). This is the 4 Ps of marketing.
- There's no reason to be pushy in your marketing. Instead, you put the information out in ways that allow the people seeking your product (a good story to read) to find that product, therefore fulfilling their needs.

CHAPTER 21
YOUR WEBSITE

It may seem to be premature, but the moment a writer decides to try to make a go of it in a business sense, they should have a website set up. While it seems awkward, because there isn't much to put on there if you haven't really been published, there are some easy ways to remedy this. One way to address this is to set up a website on a blogging platform and to get involved with the blogging community. We'll discuss that and a regular website to present options. Either way, the point of having a website early on is to give editors who scope out their writers somewhere to visit and see that they mean business. As you get published, the website will be where your readers can find you and the other work you've done.

A regular website doesn't need to be complicated at all, especially in the early part of a writing business. Let's start from the bottom and work our way up. If you have no writing credits and don't present at conferences and such, there's only a need for a main website page that introduces you and links out to any social media you want to share with others. There should be some sort of "About Me" aspect to it. This is an excellent place to include a long bio, which should already exist; a headshot, which some publishers will want upon acceptance of a story; the social media links; and something fun. An example of something fun to include is a top ten list or random facts about the author. This gives editors and readers something to check out when they come to the website. If you primarily work in one genre, there should be something representative there, such as a list of your favorite horror novels or favorite romance authors or the most interesting true crime cases. This sets up the beginning of a platform.

As you get publication and speaking credits, those can be added to the website. This is where it can be spread out across separate pages. The landing (or home) page is the most important one on a website, as it's what will be used to draw people in and make them look around the rest of the site. Any other pages should be directly linked to from the landing page. There should also be a spot for current news and updates on the front page. While appearances and publications should ultimately have their own pages, announcing these items as they come up on the landing page is also a good idea. This should take the form of some manner of news or update, and be an announcement of what the news is, with a link to the proper page for more information.

An example of this would be a publication announcement. In this case, there would be news on the landing page that proudly proclaims that a publication you're in has come out. A visual, such as the cover image, which can easily be obtained from the publisher, their website, or Amazon, should be on the front page. This is where things need to be eye catching. Underneath that photo and announcement would then be a link to the publications page, where they could find whatever you've chosen to share, such as the buy links, a blurb about the book, which story is yours, a summary of that story, and anything else that seems pertinent. All of these things don't need to be included, but the buy links absolutely do. The rest is whatever sounds good to you.

When there's only one or a couple publications on that page, adding the extra details is a good idea so there's not a bunch of white space, and so it looks busier and more involved than it necessarily is. The more publications on the tab, the simpler those listings will need to be. Once there are enough publications, especially if there are anthologies in addition to your own books, they can even be split into different pages. Make sure to stay on top of buy links; sometimes they go out of print, so the publication can either be entirely removed or the links can be removed and a note can be added saying it's out of print.

There's a separate area in this book about making appearances that will go in-depth on that topic, but for the time being, if you're interested in making appearances, it's a good idea to have a page with your contact information and what type of appearances you're willing to do. As you book appearances, those will be added to the page. Having been both an author making appearances *and* the person booking authors to make appearances, I can say that it's helpful to provide a press kit, which we'll go into more later in this section, and to either provide a summary of what you're willing to teach or a listing of past workshops so someone checking out the site to book you can get an idea of what you're qualified to speak about.

Just as with a resume, putting any sort of expertise on this page, even if it's not completely writing related, can be a help. An example of this would be if you're also a business attorney. Someone booking you as an author would also be able to consider you for business and legal workshops and panels. This can be a boost for you in terms of booking appearances. Frequently, conventions will ask what other areas of expertise you possess for exactly this reason, especially as conventions, versus conferences, aren't usually all about writing. This is a good place to address what level of nerdom you exist in, as well. Meaning, if you know all about Manga or you're into comics or you could ace a trivia night on *Doctor Who,* these are things the booking party can put into play. These items are easily ones that can be in the "About Me" section or as some sort of fun fact on the landing page.

If you suddenly get busy and/or famous, and your news is hopping, the "About Me" section can also migrate to another page. When this happens, it's important to pay attention and try to keep updates on that main page. Make sure there are visual items to pull people in. This could be book covers or photos of you at events, to name a couple options. Have interesting, engaging items on that landing page, then link to your "About Me" page so people know where to look for more information. As you can see from just these last couple pages, a website will morph over time. It will reflect where you are in your writing journey. The more you have going on, the more there is to put on a website and split out. Take a moment to be excited about it as you work to modify the website. This means you're growing as a writer!

PRESS KIT

A press or media kit is simply an area where you gather all the information you might expect to give out to various forms of media. Having it on your website allows anyone to grab the information for themselves without having to ask for it. It's convenient for both parties, because it can eliminate extraneous emails and ensure that someone putting information about you out on their website or social media can grab it without having to wait for a response to an email. Many people putting on events are volunteers, so they work when they can. Signing on to work the one day you can do it and not having a return email with information you requested is a pain in the behind.

Things to provide on your press kit:

- A choice of headshots that can be copied
- Bios of different lengths
- Any social media or other website links
- A way to contact you, such as your author email
- Accolades or awards won
- Book information if you have an upcoming or new release

HOST SELECTION

Let's take a step back and look at how to set up a website in the first place. There are plenty of inexpensive (or free) and simple ways to set up a website, all at varying levels of user capability. The blog websites make it pretty easy, specifically Blogger and Wordpress. There are also sites like Wix and Go Daddy that have website templates and aren't typically too expensive. A third option is to pay someone to set up a real website, but it will have to be taken into consideration that, unless you have some basic understanding of how to edit that website, you'll have to hire them to make changes whenever that's necessary. This can get pretty expensive. The fourth option involves having a friend or family member willing to do this work for you. If you won't be paying them, make sure you're trading in some way, even if it's a dinner out each time they have to make a change. Otherwise, they'll end up getting frustrated and pulling back. Even if you're bending over backwards to keep them happy, you could ultimately lose that help for a variety of reasons, so ensure you keep all your access information in case you need to find a replacement. This is true even for professionals you're paying.

Finding help can be tricky. If you're paying a professional to do your website, ensure you have worked out all terms in advance and have a contract. During the initial hunt for someone to do the work, it's a good idea to ask friends if they have recommendations and to otherwise research the people you're considering. Be sure to get references from the website designer that allow you to view the websites they've set up. If you don't like their websites, don't hire them. Another consideration is how much they'll charge for modifications in the future. Also, how quickly do they respond when you contact them for information? You want to be sure that they can be reached should an emergency occur.

BLOGGING

This is as good a place as any to examine using a blog to keep your website busy, especially in the early months and years of the writing journey. Blogs can be set up as websites with pages, but having the blog page be the landing page means there's more of a chance to have active information bringing people in. For a non-blog page, there are ways to program it so that updates on certain pages automatically update that main page with a teaser of some sort, but that, again, may well come down to an actual website designer and programmer. The main blog site bloggers tend to use currently is Wordpress, with Blogger also being common among writers who blog. Blogger is the simpler of the two, and more user-friendly in many ways, but that also means it has more limitations on the type of content that can be added. Wordpress involves more complicated processes, but they also have more capabilities and plug-ins. Other common blog websites include Wix, Squarespace, and Weebly. Choosing a site is something that will need to be ascertained by each individual personally, as none are really better than the others, but they are different in how they're handled.

The easiest way to decide which way to go in terms of website platforms is to check out the main web pages, look at other author's sites, look for discussions in forums about people's experiences, and to try out any free trials or free setups there may be. It's a personal choice. One thing to bear in mind is that the website can be started in the simplest way possible then eventually migrate to another platform. You could use a free site like Blogger in the beginning, and when things are rocking later on, an actual website expert can be brought in to make a more professional site. In other words, you're not stuck in one place forever, so don't put too much weight on the choice. In the beginning, it's most important to have an accessible site that's easy to update but will look professional.

DOMAIN NAME

It's a good idea to acquire your own domain name and use it as a redirect to whatever blog or website you use. This will allow later migrations without having to change the URL that's possibly been shared out, bookmarked, printed on business cards or bookmarks, etc. If that domain name can be your actual author name, perfect. It isn't always possible, though. If your name is taken as a domain already, go to that URL to check it out and see what you're up against. For example, it might not be great to have a domain name that's one letter off from a porn site. Or maybe that could work for you. Depends on what your goal is. But if the other domain is one you wouldn't want to even be accidentally associated with, adding one letter, for instance, might not be the best choice in this particular experience. But if it's not actively being used, even though someone else owns it, or it's no big deal if people accidentally end up on this wrong page first, adding your middle initial or the word "author" or something like that to the domain isn't a bad idea. There's also the consideration that yourauthorname.com may not be available, but yourauthorname.net might be. Again, not a great idea if the .com will lead somewhere bad, but not a big deal if it will just mean an extra search or something. There's also branding, such as if you're starting a press, that might make more sense than your author name. All of these considerations are valid and personal.

Some of the more trusted places to get domain names are Bluehost, GoDaddy, Domain.com, Hostgator, and Hostinger. Be sure to research anywhere you're looking for domain names and/or hosting. There are frequently tech articles online that discuss the best ones or the ones with the most bells and whistles. Forum discussions can be helpful in learning about others' experiences. This is also a great option for asking for referrals from your friends. Ask them what they like or don't like about the service they've used, how dependable the service is, if they've ever had to contact customer support and how that went, and research the pricing. Don't blindly choose one provider over another because they're the cheapest; be sure to research them first.

EMAIL ADDRESS

With a website and domain name, there are ways to set up an email address through that website. This doesn't mean it has to be done that way, but it's on the table. Your email, like your website domain name, should be personalized and easy to find and remember, if possible, which is why using your author name makes the most sense. Chances are, if they're trying to find your website, they remember your name, at the very least, and that's what they'll search on first. Having a writing email is a good idea. Just as it's preferable to have a separate work email from your home email, it's preferable to have a separate writing account, too. It's easier and it looks more professional. This email should be used for all writing-related correspondence, from submitting stories to publishers to receiving bookings for speaking opportunities. If you don't want to pay for an email or to set it up through your website, grabbing an email address with your author name from a free site, such as Gmail or MSN, is perfectly acceptable, cheap, and easy. It's a solid way to go. Understand, though, that an email with a personalized domain (the part after the @) lends credibility to you and makes it less likely newsletters and information sent out from that email will end up in spam folders.

CONCLUSION

It should go without saying, but no matter how the website and email are set up, they need to be professional, personalized, and accessible. Don't blast an editor on your website or troll news groups with your author name. You're establishing a business, and these aspects are part of that business. Personal issues should be kept to personal email addresses. Spoiler alert: this will be addressed in Chapter Twenty-Two on social media, where I'll also further address blogging and how to use it as social media.

A website can be as complicated or simple as works for the individual. Carefully consider whether it will be a website or a blog to start; what platform will work best with your aesthetics, your tech knowledge, and your time; and what domain name you intend to use from here on out. While there are instances that might require changing that domain in the future, chances are it will be one thing that stays consistent, no matter how many times a website might need to be changed. Always bear in mind that your website might be the first someone sees of you, and therefore their first impression. It will also be the place readers come to get news and to find books you're in or appearances you're going to make, plus the place editors might look to find out a bit more about this person who submitted a story they like. It will represent you as much as your stories sometimes, so make it worth it.

CHAPTER SUMMARY

- Every writer should set up a website as soon as they decide to become professional writers.
- A website can start out simply on a free site, with a single page, then grow from there as you grow as an author.
- There are free, inexpensive, and pricier options for website setup.
- Get a personalized domain name to begin with.
- Put something interesting on the landing page, such as a blog or About Me section with trivia about you.
- Even once your website has grown, because your career has, ensure there's interesting and frequently updated information on the landing page.
- Always list your publications on your website.
- Always list your appearances on your website.
- Editors and readers will use your website as a resource.

CHAPTER 22
SEO – SEARCH ENGINE OPTIMIZATION

Thris is a tough one, but it's important. You probably hear SEO tossed around all the time. It sounds like some strange creature that only a few can do successfully. In fact, there are entire jobs dedicated to SEO. But the thing about SEO is that there are varying levels of usage, and there are some basic ways you can improve your SEO on your website.

The first thing you need to know about SEO is that it's needed to get your website to show up on search engines. Search engines are programmed to search the website for pertinent links related to the search term plugged in by the user. They "crawl" the web searching for their search terms constantly, then arranging the information based on its relevance, quality, and authority. Just having a commonly searched term on your website does not mean it will be indexed or that it will have a high enough rank to show up earlier in the search results. There are quality checks it has to pass first. There are people who will flood pages with search terms rather than actual content—this is called keyword stuffing, and will actually harm your optimization now, because the search engine algorithms are getting better at weeding out spam content.

It's a good idea to research popular keywords in your domain (your genre, in writing, etc.) and decide what to write posts about based on those keywords. This way your posts address the things that are most searched about, but will be quality pieces about those keywords, rather than just a spam listing of words. Keywords and words related to them should also be included in headers, text under images, titles, URLs, and any other key areas. Again, make sure they're relevant in these places. Don't just scatter them around the page in a nonsensical way, but do stress them when it makes sense. You can use Google Keyword Planner, Ubersuggest, and Ahrefs Webmaster Tools to research keywords.

In terms of quality, the algorithms are looking for websites that are user-friendly and relevant. They want a well laid out page, with clean coding, that will resize appropriately for mobile phone users. These days, more than half of people are doing their web searches on phones instead of computers. Make sure your website is mobile friendly. An easy way to do this is to pull it up on your own phone and see how it works. If it resizes so the whole page fits on the screen, rather than zooming in on one area without you doing so manually, you should be good to go. Try this on a variety of machines and screen sizes if you have them. For example, a tablet screen is different, and you want your website showing up correctly in that format. Many people use voice searches, too, so think of key phrases someone might use when speaking aloud versus typing it out.

The algorithms are also looking for sites that are updated frequently and therefore remain relevant for the search terms. This is why having a blog or some sort of regularly updated content connected to your website is important. As long as that blog is getting updated, the website it's connected to is more likely to be ranked higher. The content has to be useful and relevant, which means it's also more likely to be shared out on social media and linked to on other people's websites. These backlinks are valuable, though the website backlinks are far more valuable than social media backlinks. If someone shares a link to your blog post or article on their blog or website, that creates something like a trail that will make the search engines more likely to find it. A link being shared out shows the algorithm that this is something of value. The more backlinks are created to your site, the more relevant it becomes to search engines. This is why it's important to have some manner of real, valuable content on your website. Not only does it bring readers to you, but it may also end up bringing search engines to you.

A great way to get backlinks is to write useful content for others' blogs and do post exchanges with another blogger, meaning each of you guest post on the other person's blog. Some other options would be to participate in blog hops and participate in other blogger-author's blog tours, meaning you or they do a blog post about their new release, and they link to the bloggers participating by sharing their information. These will net backlinks that prove your website is trustworthy to the search engine algorithms. The problem with the latter two options are that they will net backlinks, but the posts are usually going to be advertising ones, not quality content ones. The hope is to get traffic to your site that will visit your more quality posts and hopefully create those more useful backlinks to those.

These backlinks from other websites aren't the only ones that matter. Search engines will also take note if you link to other pages on your own site. This is where it comes in handy to have multiple pages on a website. Say you post about an upcoming event. You can do a post about it and link to your "Appearances" tab in that post. Be sure to put the name of the page in the link, rather than saying something like "click here." It makes it a more relevant link in terms of searches.

How much people comment on your blog can also impact how it appears in the search engines. The more comments on a post, the more valuable it's thought that post is. Taking all these measures into consideration and making a blog and website that people make it a point to visit, with consistently relevant information, will also give your site authority. Authority increases your standing in SEO, as well. Basically, you're trying to improve your website in enough ways to ensure they all work together to bring visitors to your site through a variety of means, engage them, and encourage them to share links to your site, so your standing improves. Round and round you go. This is an ongoing task, as the algorithms have been made to learn and improve how they find and index sites for the search engines.

In general, you're looking to create a web presence that provides useful, interesting content that will convey what you need it to convey while also catching the attention of search engine algorithms. The information and features, or the content, should be aligned in such a way as to be consistent across the use of titles, subheadings, captions, lists, and keywords in the text. The information that surrounds the keywords is what tells the algorithms the context behind the content on the page. If you think about it, one word can mean many different things. In order to understand what context that word has, there must be other words around it to further define it. Search engines look for all the details, not just individual words. In this way, the algorithm knows that when you mention a grasshopper, the other content surrounding that single word will describe whether it's an insect or an alcoholic beverage. All facets of your page play into this, so if you have an article about a grasshopper and there's a photo on the page that goes with the article, that photo needs a caption that says it's a grasshopper, plus a title that pertains to the content. It all works together.

Understand that this is an incredibly simplified explanation of SEO and what you need to do to make it work for you. My intention is to get you started with some basic knowledge of it. As your career expands, you should do more research on it and learn more and better ways to improve your ranking on search engines. On-page optimization is made up of the things you can personally do on your web page to increase your SEO standings. Off-page optimization involves the backlinks and exterior links to your content. Researching these more thoroughly should bring useful knowledge to help expand your optimization.

CHAPTER SUMMARY

- SEO is important in terms of getting your website to show up on search engines.
- Search engine algorithms are looking for relevance, quality, and authority, as well as context.
- Use keywords, but don't abuse them.
- Backlinks can help improve SEO.
- Updating and interaction are important to get and keep search engine attention.

CHAPTER 23
SOCIAL MEDIA

I n this day and age, having a website is vital, but social media is also valuable. Part of the problem with social media is there are constantly new platforms popping up and reader attention may be drawn to different places as they tire of one platform and move to another. In addition, different groups are drawn to different platforms, and even those groups switch their loyalties at the drop of a hat. It can seem overwhelming when trying to figure out social media for a professional appearance, but the simplest rule is to choose the platform you're most comfortable with and focus on that one. If there's a form of social media you'll never use, it's probably best not to try to force it by signing up for it. Where this becomes an issue is when your primary audience gravitates to a form of social media you'd prefer not to use. When that happens, you've got a decision to make. On the one hand, it's valuable to be where your readers are. On the other, if you're forcing yourself to use a platform you don't enjoy or don't understand, that will be conveyed to the people following you on that platform, which diminishes how useful your presence there will be.

On any social media platform, it's important to fill out your profile information in a way that keeps it up to date and gets the information you prefer out there. It doesn't take long to do this, and it gives people a place to check out your information. Your social media should be networked as much as possible, meaning you should connect different forms of social media, plus your website, by linking to them where it makes sense. For example, your profile on any form of social media should have a link to your website. Everything should point back to your website, at a minimum, because that's your home base and the place you'll have the most information available. Having a good representative photo, preferably a professional headshot, is important, as well. People don't connect with random images or cartoon representations. They want to see your face. It forges a better connection.

Another good rule of thumb for social media is to follow the 80/20 rule. By this I mean that your actual promotion should only make up about twenty percent of your content. This is a good ratio for all the social media platforms. Having eighty percent content, including promoting other writers, means you're more likely to appeal to more people who will follow or friend you. It shows your account is not just self-promotion all the time. Nobody follows an account to be constantly sold to. The secret is finding just the right mix to promote yourself while entertaining people and networking the rest of the time. People who do more than twenty percent promotion are seen as pushy and uninteresting.

FACEBOOK

Facebook still manages to be the primary platform used by authors, but its effectiveness has been waning for years. Middle-aged folks (ages 30 to 65), especially women, tend to hang out here still, and they have significant buying power. The problem is that, despite them still having a lot of users, engagement has started going down. At the same time, Facebook has been making it harder for businesses to get attention to their pages without paying for that attention. Their algorithms squash things like posts with links in them and anything coming from a business page. Unfortunately, Facebook still appears to be a necessary evil until more people have found a better alternative, which means it's still a strong contender for being in the top platforms used by authors to get their names out there. At least if the middle-aged crowd is part of your audience. And as middle-aged buyers are a large portion of the book market, chances are they're part of your audience.

More than the other platforms, Facebook's rules seem to change the most rapidly. As soon as authors adapt to one change, like no longer putting links in their main posts, they get swatted another way and have to adapt again. This means being tapped into author communities or business communities is a must. Engagement on social media bumps you up in algorithms, which means the types of posts need to be those that at least illicit "likes," but much better is posting something that will get shared and commented on. This can involve asking questions or posting memes. Making your own memes with your name or URL somewhere on them can be a good way to get shares and maybe draw eyes to your website.

There are basically three ways you can interact on Facebook right now: personal page, business page, and group. A personal page requires connecting with someone via friending, though people can also follow your page without being friends with you. This means your public posts will appear in their newsfeed. Those posts that are not public, they won't be able to see. These sorts of pages, which are the default, are typically those that someone has setup to interact with friends and family, but many end up friending fellow writers, publishers, editors, and folks of that nature on their personal pages. It's where most people post the most often. However, this page won't necessarily lead to many book sales outside of actual friends and family, and the algorithm can be skewed if your friends and family are likely to click through, but not read that sort of book. While fellow authors might buy books, most are saturated with authors on their page and can't buy everything that pops up in their timeline. This type of page is best for networking with fellow writers and professionals, not so much for sales. Your interactions here will determine whether the algorithms share your posts much, so it needs to be a reciprocal agreement, where you like and comment on others' posts. The more interaction you have, the more others can see your posts.

The business page used to be the way to go. For this one, it should be set up under your author name. It typically gets created under your primary personal page. People "like" this page and follow it. They aren't friends so that you'll be able to see what they're posting. It's a one-way street, unlike the personal page, which is a two-way street. This is a good way to have a public-facing Facebook page that you give out on your website and publications, so fans of your writing have a way to follow you. All news should be shared on this page, such as publications, upcoming appearances, etc. This is also a good place to link video of appearances that have already happened. You can pin a single important post to the top of this type of page, so if you've got a story out in a new anthology, that news can be pinned so anyone visiting your page will see it. Unfortunately, this is the area of Facebook that appears to have taken the biggest hit as they try to monetize Facebook more, which means that even though people intentionally like and follow you, they're still not seeing your business page posts in their feeds much. Again, the more engagement and interaction that occurs on this page, the more people will see it. Share things that people will share, such as memes that might lead people back to you. This is a good place to post calls to action, such as asking people to review a book you're in.

Groups are replacing business pages, but this means people have to join the group to see posts in it. Usually, groups allow for postings from anyone in the group, though any page or group you setup has settings that can be modified to your preferences. These types of pages still require interaction, but for the time being, they're more likely to show up in people's feeds if they've joined the group. If you can have fun activities and interactions with people, such as posting interesting news in addition to your own news, engagement might increase. Groups are good for reader groups or to set up a street team, which is basically a group of your readers who help get the word out about your books.

There's also a way to pay for sponsored ads on Facebook. This is something worth researching online to see if it would work for you. Many find it costs more than it brings in, but this means they're not targeting the proper audiences. It may take quite a bit of tweaking to make it worthwhile. When done incorrectly, ads mostly go to people who already have you on their friend list or who have already liked your page or joined your group, which means they should have already organically seen your information if Facebook wasn't squelching those posts in the first place. On the other hand, some people swear by Facebook ads. The thing here is to set up a compelling ad with a visual that grabs people's attention, plus a call to action, which, in this case, is to buy the book. Calls to action work better than passive advertising. A call to action promotes completing a specific action, like buying a book, liking a page, or sharing something. People are more likely to do these things if they're directly asked to do it. Be sure to figure out who you need to target, who your most likely readers are, before trying ads. This may lead to more successful marketing.

Something to note is that it's bad form to run around "friending" people on Facebook, then instantly sending them requests to like your pages or buy your books. This turns people off and is considered hard selling by most. Instead of ending in a sale for you, it's more likely to end in being blocked. While it may seem like a wasted opportunity, being blocked by someone who might have otherwise bought a book they saw on your page later on is definitely a wasted opportunity, and people have become more likely to post the names of people who do this as a call out to alert others it might happen to them. It happens a lot on the personal pages of authors. They'll happily share that there's a newbie running around in virtual space, being rude and trying to hard sell the people on their friend list. This means you risk losing more than that one person if you drop into their DMs with a sales pitch.

Another no-no is to post an advertisement or link onto someone else's page. There's always someone who friends other writers just to try to advertise on their pages. Again, this can get you blocked or even blacklisted. Bear in mind, too, that many authors are friends with editors and agents they've worked with, which means your bad behavior won't be kept to just a group of authors who weren't going to buy your books, anyway. It might be seen by editors you'd like to submit to down the line. Lo and behold, your name pops up in their emails, and they've already seen poor behavior from you online. Would a manager at a company hire you if they saw you on a friend's page flipping off your boss behind their back in a selfie? Probably not.

The same applies here. If they've seen you might be a pain to work with or that your bad name might drag down their own publication or bring other issues out later on, they're more likely to skip working with you. Don't be that person. None of us like that person.

Finally, in terms of Facebook, a medium level of activity is good. If you're never on Facebook, so only post once in a blue moon, no one's going to see that post, because you haven't been interacting. The algorithms will kill you here. Posting a couple things each day is a good idea. If you go overboard and post fifty things, chances are you'll be unfollowed or unfriended. You have to find a happy medium that works for you. You should post things other than advertisements for yourself, for the most part. If you do a post advertising a release, that should be accompanied at some point that day by something fun, like a meme or link to an interesting article, and maybe something about a goofy thing that happened to you that day. You're sandwiching your advertisements between content people are more interested in. This way, people don't unfollow or block you, because all you do is try to get them to buy things. There's a skill to marketing that takes a long time to get down, but not being annoying would be the number one way to start getting there. People want content. That content will hopefully make them open to the advertisements when they do come.

TWITTER

Moving onto Twitter, this one has long appealed to a younger crowd, but it's also fading away into social media obscurity. Many older folks avoid it, because it feels like you're shouting into the void, and it involves more frequent posting in order to be useful. While Twitter trended younger before, people are increasingly leaving the platform behind. It's become a political hotbed, as has Facebook, and is most popular among business-to-business users. Still, Twitter has its uses for authors, including networking with other writing professionals and advertising your wares. There are also ways to pitch your books during certain periods, as well as to find out what editors and agents are looking for. These are the things that are most useful on Twitter versus other platforms.

One of the things about Twitter that it's important to note is that it matters how many followers you have versus how many users you're following. The numbers are visible to anyone, and since the beginning, it's been considered to look more successful if your followers outnumber your follows. If you have more followers, it shows that all those people found you compelling enough to follow. On the other hand, if you follow more than follow you, it looks like you ran around following everyone without discernment, but that few of them chose to follow you back. Don't automatically follow back everyone who follows you. Instead, be sure to check out their accounts and make sure that they appear to be 1) a valid user, not a spammer or bot, 2) someone you're interested in following, and 3) not posting things that bother you, such as if all their tweets are political and that's not something you'd enjoy. Note that there are users who will follow everyone they can, wait until that person follows them back, then unfollow them. These people are collecting followers, and aren't actually interested in interacting with you. While you don't get a notification every time someone unfollows you, there's a site that will track it for you. To get there, go to *who.unfollowed.me*. The site will have you sign in via your Twitter account, and will track both new followers and those who have unfollowed your account. I try to go through the site about once per month and unfollow those who've unfollowed me. This also removes unnecessary posts from your feed.

Twitter is huge on interaction. This means the more you do in Twitter, the more you'll get out of it. It can be a major time sink, so plan accordingly. It may be easier to use a scheduling platform like Hootsuite, Later, Buffer, or Sprout Social so you can spend one day pre-scheduling social media posts instead of having to pop in multiple times per day. We'll go more into detail about scheduling platforms later in this section. With Twitter, it's important to not only post frequently, but to also "like" and retweet others' posts. It's also polite to thank someone for an RT (retweet) by tweeting them a thank you. A tweet can be pinned to the top of your profile, which keeps it at the top of your feed. It also gives people an automatic post to retweet should they want to do so. Often, it's nice to reciprocate a retweet of one of your posts by retweeting a post from the other person's feed.

Twitter introduced the idea of hashtags (#) to categorize tweets and catch the right kind of attention. There are many ways writers can use hashtags to their advantage. It's easy to search hashtags relevant to what you're looking for, but specific to writers there are a bunch that can come in handy. A good rule of thumb is to not use more than three hashtags in a tweet, which you'll find is quite different when we get to Instagram and their use of hashtags. Also important is the fact that hashtags cannot contain spaces; they must be one word, though each word can be capitalized. One way to use a hashtag to be involved with others is to tweet about books you're reading and use the hashtag #AmReading. You can also do a search on the hashtag to see what other people are posting and like their tweets. For writers, there's also the hashtag #AmWriting, which can be used to tweet about things like word counts, a funny typo, or whatever writing-related adventures you've had. #TeaserTues gives you a place to throw out a line from your manuscript as a teaser. In addition, you can always hashtag your genre.

In terms of connecting with agents and editors, the big hashtag is #MSWL. It stands for Manuscript Wish List. This hashtag is a good one to search to see what editors and agents are tweeting about wanting to see. Use this to find places to submit or query. Other hashtags that can come in useful for getting honest feedback from willing agents and editors are #AskAgent and #AskEditor. There are also events that open for limited times: #PitchWars and #PitMad. Search online to see when they're active, then tweet out your pitch with the appropriate hashtags.

The various hashtags can fill an entire book, so I won't go into too much detail here, but a final round of hashtags are those that bring together communities for fun and games. Tweet out a challenge to write one thousand words in one hour with #1K1H, and connect with others who take up the challenge with you. Or you can simply tweet out that you're writing for the next little while and use #WritingSprint to see if others will join you. Use #LitChat on Mondays, Wednesdays, and Fridays to talk with fellow writers. If you want to bring attention to some of your followers and possibly get them new followers, do a tweet on Fridays saying why these people are great and using their Twitter handles (@theirhandle) with #followfriday or #ff.

These hashtags are a good start. Look up different types of writing related hashtags and figure out what sounds fun to you to do. If you participate with just a couple of these, you're sure to connect with plenty of other writers and hopefully widen your horizons on Twitter. Again, it comes down to reciprocity and networking here. Yes, you should absolutely be tweeting out your releases on Twitter. In fact, you can do it more on Twitter than on Facebook, because Twitter moves so fast that it's less likely to look like spam and more likely to find an audience the more you tweet it out. Look for a good balance still between content and advertisements. If your feed is entirely advertising, people are less likely to follow you. They want content, just as on Facebook. The more content and the less advertising, the better to get your brand out there and find followers. I personally don't tweet advertisements more than about once per week, and usually less than that. But I'm not a great tweeter in the first place. Follow authors you're interested in and see what they're tweeting. If it seems like a good balance to you, it's a good idea to try to use that in your own tweet life balance.

INSTAGRAM

The next big one is Instagram. It's all about pictures, images, and now videos. A lot of people fed up with social media vitriol have been flocking to Instagram, where it's easier to scroll through and see interesting things, rather than getting caught up in toxic exchanges. And unlike with Twitter, the more hashtags the merrier. Just don't do more than thirty hashtags in a single post or your caption will be removed. A handy thing about the hashtags is popular options will pop up as you start to type out the hashtag and phrase. It will even tell you how popular it is by how many are using it. If you're not sure what hashtags to use, just start typing out things that seem relevant and see what autofills, then select that thing. Remember that hashtags must be all one word, with no spaces. However, underscores can be used as well, such as with #writers_of_instagram. Know that it isn't frequently used, so unless an autofill suggestion comes up that shows it's popular, it's best to keep it to one nonstop word.

A lot of the hashtags used on Twitter are also used on Instagram, and just as with Twitter, it's easy to look up some of the more popular hashtags for writers. Hashtagging a post gets it seen by people who don't follow you, and it can even get you on the general "front page" of Instagram, which can expand who's seeing it. Using hashtags is a good way to get new followers and to connect with like-minded people. With Instagram, you're less likely to put in frequent writing and marketing content, though you should absolutely be mixing that in, and more likely to post photos you've taken that day, an interesting meal, pictures of your pets, videos of you doing goofy things or discussing book topics, and selfies. The more you hashtag, the more you get out there. Using hashtags like #bookstagram and #amreading can connect you with readers, so be sure to experiment with the different hashtags out there and see what you come up with. You can also follow popular hashtags to get those posts in your feed. If you have a hashtag that might be questionable, look it up to be sure it doesn't lead somewhere darker than you might like or inappropriate. You don't want to hashtag something you post and have it lead to porn or a hunting trophy site if that's not what you intended.

The thing about Instagram is that it encourages creativity. Don't just post a picture of your book. Instead, set up a whole visual treat by arranging decorations around it or putting it in a place that lets it stand out. For example, if you write horror and there's a neat craggy tree near you, put your book on a branch and photograph it. If you've got a hobby that's easy to photograph, share that, as well. Are you a hiker? Share pictures of nature out on your hikes. There's a lot that can be done on Instagram, and it can be quite fun. Just be sure to remember what you're using it for and occasionally post promotional posts. Also, ask questions in your posts. This is actually a good idea across social media. Asking questions might net answers, which boosts you in the algorithms due to the interactions occurring on your posts. When you get answers, "like" them at the very least, or respond if there's something to say. This boosts you even more.

Instagram used to be for just your phone, but it can now be used on the computer. This has simplified being able to schedule posts. In addition, if you have both a Facebook and an Instagram account, you can tie them together using the Business Suite, which is available on Facebook business pages. You can then schedule out posts for both Facebook and Instagram from one place. Sharing other people's posts is also different on Instagram, but it is possible.

TIKTOK

TikTok is rapidly becoming a popular place for authors. It's video-based, so rather than just passively posting pictures, you're expected to make videos. As with Twitter and Instagram, hashtags are widely used in this format, as well. #booktok is trending significantly, which means if you can hashtag a video of you recommending someone else's books or reviewing them, you can hit a wide audience. TikTok moves fast, as newer social media formats often do, so following trends is important here. Try to incorporate hashtags that are trending and that work for your personal author platform so you can remain in the flow and be seen by others. The best way to learn these platforms is to sign up and play around with them a bit. It's also a good idea to look up articles on how best to use them. There's a ton of information out there, right at your fingertips. There's no reason to flail about and struggle

BLOGGING

Another form of social media is a blog. Again, this can double as your website, but if it's used as a blog in any way, there are rules of thumb to follow. Just as with any other social media, interaction matters. It's not just about writing blog posts and letting them flap in the wind. Instead, you need to engage in the writing and reading blogging community and interact with other bloggers. This means reading their posts and commenting on them. It can also mean sharing out their posts on social media, which they may reciprocate. There are ways to follow different kinds of blogs that will get the updates sent to you or allow you to be notified, so look into that for whatever platform you're using and they're using. There's a lot that can be learned on some blogs. There's also a great sense of community if you're actively participating.

While blogging reached its peak and started to fade, the writing community is still quite active in the blogosphere. There are things called blog hops and blog fests that people partake in, which can be weekly, monthly, or annual. Some examples of these are the A-to-Z Challenge, which happens once per year, in April. For this challenge, participants are asked to post every day except Sunday, with posts themed in alphabetical order. There's a large portion of bloggers that participate each year, and it's a good way to get some exposure, especially if you not only post but hop around to other participating blogs to comment on their posts. This challenge can be accessed at the website www.a-to-zchallenge.com. An easier way to participate in the challenge is to preload your posts by writing them in advance and scheduling them to appear on the correct days.

A monthly challenge writers can participate in is the Insecure Writer's Support Group, or IWSG. This was created by Alex J. Cavanaugh and occurs the first Wednesday of each month. Participants write about their insecurities, write encouragement to other writers, inspire other writers, or answer the optional question of the month. This is another hop where participants are encouraged to post, but also to visit other participants. It's another fun way to connect with others and build your writing community. Those who don't participate as required will be removed from the lists, so it should never be used purely for promotion. The point of participating in challenges like these isn't direct promotion, but engaging in a community that will support you through your writing endeavors and even your personal struggles. Those who participate are brought into a welcoming and supportive community. This challenge can be accessed at www.insecurewriterssupportgroup.com.

A fun and creative challenge occurs every other month. The WEP Challenge, or "Write, Edit, Publish," gives a prompt, which people can create a piece of writing to. In addition, participants can get feedback by posting what type of feedback they're interested in. Again, this hop is about community, and participants can't just sign up and not actually participate. There are specific dates for the posts, and there is a word limit. There's even a winner, a second place, and an encouragement award, which come with badges to display on your blog. This challenge can be found at www.writeeditpublishnow. blogspot.com.

The more involved in the blogging community you are, the more you will find out about other types of hops and activities you can participate in. There are usually linky lists to sign up on at a specific website, with dates of posting outlined. There will also be rules for each challenge or hop. It can be a lot of fun, but also time consuming, so be sure to pick and choose the ones you're most interested in. All hops are intended to provide interaction, which means visiting the other participants, commenting, and sharing their posts on social media if you really liked them. The hope is that this will also be done for your posts at some point, but that's not guaranteed. The best way to get that type of support is to be a genuine member of the writer blogging community and interact with and support others. Those who participate only to promote themselves will not find they're fully engaged in the community, and therefore won't get that support.

In terms of topics to blog about, this should be geared toward something you're comfortable talking about regularly. Theming it toward your genre(s) is also a good idea. If you're a romance author, talk about romance-related things. It doesn't have to be all books all the time. It can be movies, real-life stories, and whatever else you can loosely tie into your writing career. You can also post about writing-related things in terms of what you're doing that your readers may be interested in. Blog about where you are in the business, things you've learned, news you've read, and whatever else is pertinent. If you've got hobbies, you can wrap those in. Travel a lot? Post pictures and adventure stories. The important thing is to post about things you find interesting that will also hopefully interest your readers.

It's a good idea to set a regular schedule and post it on your blog. While bloggers used to be expected to post multiple times per week, that has slowed down, changing the expectations. However, readers will expect some sort of schedule. If you can post once per month, stick to that and make it the same day each month. If you can post once per week, pick a day of the week to post. Tuesdays, Wednesdays, or Thursdays tend to be best for blog traffic. Sometimes it helps to have theme days, and that schedule can be placed up, as well. For example, maybe the second week of each month you post reviews of what you've been reading. You might then do a genre post the third week of each month. If you're doing themes, set the schedule, and therefore the expectations, and stick to your schedule. It's sometimes easier to spend a day writing up and pre-scheduling posts at the beginning of the month.

Of course, none of it matters if you're not advertising your stories and books. Your news should always be shared on your blog, whether you're using it as a website or just a blog. You can either do special blog posts with announcements or add the announcements to your already scheduled posts. They're more likely to be seen if they're done with a post on a regular schedule. There's also no rule saying you can't do both, but the most effective way to do it is to post the news on whatever post tends to get the most traffic on your normal schedule. Blogging platforms usually provide areas where you can check for traffic and learn when people are visiting your posts the most.

It's a good idea to trade traffic with other bloggers. One way to have a reciprocal relationship that benefits both parties is to sign up to help other bloggers/writers get out information about new releases. The blogger with the new release will usually share the blogs of the people hosting them for the book release, which can lead traffic to the person sharing that news. At the same time, posting someone else's publication news on your blog might lead some of your followers to the author with the release. In addition, helping people out this way will typically lead to them being willing to do the same when you have a release.

Something to bear in mind that isn't an issue with other forms of social media is the fact that a lot of prose on a page needs to be broken up with images, lists, headers, and subheaders, especially on a screen. Even though a blog is a long form of writing, it's best to keep posts shorter in order to keep reader attention, as well as to try to post some visuals. Posts should be no more than about 1500 to 2000 words. This makes them long enough to have actual content, but short enough to keep attention in a space where attention spans are minimal. When participating in a hop where a lot of people are participating, keeping it to under 1000 words might be optimal, because people have a lot of reading to do to get through all the posts. However, in terms of SEO (search engine optimization), the posts longer than 1500 words are going to be easier to optimize.

SCHEDULING PLATFORMS

There are a gazillion other forms of social media, but it would take an entire book to cover them all, and even then, there'd be new ones to cover. Instead, let's talk about platforms used to schedule social media. Hootsuite is the better known of these, but as with many popular platforms of any kind, they change once they have enough customers in an attempt to further monetize their services. Because of this, Hootsuite is rapidly losing popularity, while other platforms are gaining it. Currently, the free version only supports two social media platforms, so while they can be used for Facebook, LinkedIn, Twitter, Instagram, Pinterest, and YouTube, the free version only allows users to set up two social media accounts to post to. It also limits how many posts can be scheduled at a time to five, and allows only one user. Despite this, it's free and a familiar platform, and it can be worth it to have that little bit of help if you don't want to schedule out a ton of posts. There are also paid plans with them that increase the number of accounts, users, and posts that can be scheduled, so it's worth looking into those paid accounts.

Slack Social is a newer platform, but it has a much better free plan than Hootsuite. They don't limit the social media accounts you can attend to and the post limit is fifty per day. The social media platforms they supported upon last checking were Facebook, Twitter, Instagram, LinkedIn, Telegram, Reddit, Blogger, and Tumblr. Another platform is Later, which allows what they call one social set, which is one account each on Facebook, Twitter, Instagram, Pinterest, TikTok, and LinkedIn. They allow ten posts per social media format on their free account. These are just a few of the platforms for scheduling social media posts. A scheduling platform like these can lessen the burden of posting to social media by allowing you to pre-schedule your posts in one sitting. The thing about social media is that it's easy to get dragged in and distracted from work if you have to keep jumping onto it, so prescheduling via a platform keeps you off social media when you don't need or want to be there and limits the time spent. Most platforms offer a free option, and they typically allow a free trial for their paid plans. Check them out and see which one works best for you and has the bells and whistles you're seeking.

CONCLUSION

Chances are, you already have forms of social media you're comfortable with. Going with those forms first means not having to learn a different type of social media while you're trying to get your author platform set up. Adding in other forms depending upon where your audience is can happen when you've established accounts for your writing persona on the familiar ones, though it's definitely important to eventually consider those that cater most to your audience. There are many resources online for the optimal workings of each form of social media, including length of posts, frequency of posting, and platform-specific options, such as hashtags. It's worth it to do the research and utilize the social media form at its optimal level of functionality. Doing it wrong or inconsistently wastes time, and your displeasure or lack of knowledge shows.

Some authors who are doing websites and various forms of social media right are:

- Website – Stephen King (stephenking.com), the Dr. Seuss website (Seussville.com), and Taylor Jenkins Reid (taylorjenkinsreid.com)

- Blog – Joanna Penn (thecreativepenn.com), Chrys Fey (writewithfey.com), and John Pistelli (johnpistelli.com)

- Facebook – Neil Gaiman (facebook.com/neilgaiman), Amy Tan (facebook.com/authoramytan), and Mindy Kaling (facebook.com/officialmindykaling)

- Twitter – Paulo Coelho (@paulocoelho), Joe Dunthorne (@joedunthorne), and Celeste Ng (@prounced_ing)

- Instagram – Jon Krakauer (@krakauernotwriting), Rupi Kaur (@rupikaur_), and Elizabeth Acevedo (@acevedowrites)

- TikTok – Chloe Gong (@thechloegong), Aiden Thomas (@aidenschmaiden), and Preeti Chhibber (@runwithskizzers)

With any form of social media you end up using, it's important to have accounts set up specifically as writing accounts. That means if you have a personal Twitter account already, a new one would need to be created for your writing-related posts. If you already have a solid following on your personal account, you can always share the social media from your professional accounts on your personal accounts, but they should go out on the professional accounts first. Set up each account to its fullest, with the profile information filled out and a professional-looking photo. Interlink the accounts and always link back to your website. Use discretion and professionalism on your social media accounts, as everything thrown out on the internet is forever. Even a post you delete later can be screenshotted or found in archives. Remember that you're representing your professional persona, and behave like you would if you were representing a company you worked for. Or better, depending upon how much you respect the company you work for.

The point in social media is outreach and networking. It can bring in customers and it can create community. It's tricky to balance a social media presence with time to write, edit, and submit stories, and each person must find their own balance with it. However, it's vital to remember that, while social media presence is important, it doesn't matter if there's no writing output. Pre-scheduling at least some posts can help. Planning out a schedule can also help. Make sure you focus on the forms you're most comfortable with and never put your social media over your writing if you can help it. A writer writes.

CHAPTER SUMMARY

- Interaction is vital on social media. Don't just post and run. Ask questions, post fun things, reply to those who comment, and like their responses. Visit other people's social media.
- Brand all social media together and link to your website.
- Fill out the profile on your social media.
- Use hashtags on Twitter, Instagram, and TikTok.
- Author groups on Facebook work better for getting your posts in front of readers than author pages or personal profiles.
- Go with your strengths on social media; don't try to be on every format.
- Consider a scheduling platform so you can schedule out social media posts once per week and not spend all your time on the various platforms.
- Follow the 80/20 rule: 80% interesting content, 20% product/selling content.
- Facebook is big with the middle-aged group, but TikTok is rapidly taking over in popularity for all age groups.
- Blogging helps you connect with both readers and the writing community.

CHAPTER 24
NEWSLETTERS

Ah, newsletters. One of the many banes of our existence, yet also something we need to have. Nobody seems to be able to come to an agreement on how often a newsletter needs to go out and what needs to be on it. It's a question I see people asking a lot. The beauty of a newsletter is that you're speaking to people who care enough about your book news to have signed up for your newsletter. Go in with that understanding and it might help make it less stressful. Newsletters allow you to communicate with those who want to hear your updates without being foiled by algorithms the way you may be with social media.

There are two main newsletter sites that have free plans in addition to paid plans: Mailchimp and Mailerlite. However, there are now other lesser-known services that offer better free plans, such as Sendinblue and EmailOctopus, who allow for more subscribers/contacts than Mailchimp and Mailerlite. Consider all the options offered by the different sites, though, as there may be benefits you prefer on one site over another. When you're just beginning, you probably won't have such a massive contact list that those subscriber minimums will impact you. As with anything else we've discussed, look at their websites, read articles about people's experiences with them, and figure out what platform will work best for you.

Newsletters work better if you're consistent with them. If there are pauses too big or it's too inconsistent, people might forget they signed up for your newsletter in the first place. So when you're deciding what frequency to use on sending your newsletter to your subscribers, first figure out what you can do consistently. Short story authors won't likely have weekly announcements unless they're self-publishing a weekly story, so monthly or quarterly will probably make the most sense. If you can manage monthly, that's probably better than quarterly, simply because quarterly newsletters are pretty far apart. But again, what's most important is how often you can commit to them.

Now we get to how you tempt people to sign up. One way is to take a sign-up sheet to any events or appearances you do. This can be a literal piece of paper or a tablet or machine with a link to the sign up that they can do right there. This isn't going to be effective until you've reached a point where you're attending events as a speaker, panelist, reader, or signer, though. Before then, you should go through the steps for the site you decide to go with that will allow you to put a sign-up form directly on your website and/or blog. The main sites all provide easy ways and instructions to do this, and they can either be linked to or embedded. Then there are always calls on social media. This is probably the least effective method, because your reach is limited by algorithms, and people on social media won't necessarily click through to sign up for something.

This is as good a place as any to make an ethical note: do not sign people up for your newsletter unless they have specifically approved it. Putting someone on your list who has not requested you do so is dishonest and is spam. If they live in Europe, you'd be violating the GDPR, which can have serious consequences. GDPR stands for General Data Protection Regulation, a European Union regulation that protects data and privacy. In addition, don't sell or give your list to anyone else. It's bad form and a violation of the trust the subscriber put in you. On that note, there are people who exchange their mailing lists. I'm not comfortable with this, so I don't do it, even though it might mean I could have more subscribers. I'd rather keep my list to people who actually want to hear from me. As such, this is an area where I will not be making any suggestions.

Something you *can* do to get more subscribers is to offer a free story to anyone who signs up or to offer some other incentive. You might do pushes on your website with an offer of a discount code for an anthology or something along those lines. Just be sure to actually deliver whatever you've promised. One thing about this is you might be more likely to lose the people who signed up for the freebie, but there may also be plenty who stay even after getting the free item. It's worth it, despite the possibly low retention rate. Every subscriber is a possible purchaser in the future.

Now, what should you write about? I've found that a mix of personal and professional works well for me and my subscribers. The sky's the limit on various bits of news you can share, so figure out what you're most comfortable with and have the time to do. Try subscribing to authors who interest you and see how you feel about what they're sharing.

Some possibilities:

- News about acceptances and releases
- Updates on appearances
- Fellow writer release news
- Links to interesting articles
- What you've done in your personal life since the last newsletter (that you're comfortable sharing)
- Interesting tidbits about recent stories you've been working on (for example, anything weird or funny you had to research)
- Guest articles
- Articles written by you
- Free content like a poem or flash fiction
- Media you've been taking in (favorite TV shows, movies, books, podcasts, etc.).

The point is to offer things that will be interesting to read about and keep them engaged, while also keeping them updated about your upcoming stories, new releases, and appearances. I've tried a variety of things, but it's boiled down to me doing a write up of what's going on in my regular life to the extent I'm willing to share, putting sections for each new release and upcoming appearance, including links for any blog posts or guest posts I think they may be interested in, and including photos since photography is a hobby of mine. Be cautious about too many photos or images, though, as they can make the newsletter load more slowly and possibly deter some folks from opening it at all. If I've done an appearance and there's a photo, I'll share that, too. For me, the newsletter is intended to be a more intimate form of communication with my readers.

Whatever the content of the newsletter, try to offset things visually by using different boxes, images, headings, colors, and anything else that will make it easy for someone to look through and find whatever content they're interested in. They may only want the new release information or to see if you're going to a specific event. Make it easy so they don't get frustrated and give up on opening your newsletter in the future. However, be cautious about making it too gaudy or unpleasant on the eyes. There can be minor changes that still set sections apart without having one be neon yellow and another bright red. You want everything to be distinctive without it being an eyesore. Make sure if you change the color of the background that the color of the font stands out. If there will be hyperlinks in that color, you may need to change the background color or the hyperlink color to ensure the hyperlink doesn't end up being the same or a similar color that fades into the background. To further your branding, matching the newsletter colors to your website is a good idea. Once again, this sends a uniform message to your readers and visually aligns everything.

Relating to the visual appeal of the newsletter, include images where necessary. If you released a story in an anthology, be sure to share the cover image of the book. If you're making an appearance at an event and the event or the creator of the event has a logo or other visual, share that visual with the link. You should also streamline the newsletter so it's not a crazy, unpleasant jumble. Try to think about what it will look like on a computer screen and a phone screen. With heavier content, I like to do dual columns. If it's a shorter, simpler newsletter, then one long, wide column will work, as long as it's not too wide. It's easier to scroll up and down than to have to go side to side.

If you're posting a book release or appearance, or anything else like that, be sure to include a link to it so people can go directly from your newsletter to the place you wish to send them. Include a call to action to buy the book or sign up for the workshop. Also be sure to include links to your website and social media, usually in or near the footer. This is how you tie your newsletter in with the rest of your presence or platform, and all those things should be used to point people to your newsletter sign up.

No one will read your content if you don't have a compelling subject line. Try to make it something engaging that pulls the reader's attention and makes them want to open the email. Don't keep the same or a similar subject line unless there's an interesting theme to it and it informs as to what's in the newsletter in some way. If you choose to use emojis in it, keep them to a minimum. Don't put the title in all capitals or put twenty exclamation points in. In short, make it an interesting subject line, and not one that looks like a text you might receive.

Your newsletter will probably grow and change as you do the same as an author. Don't be afraid to make changes if fewer people are opening your newsletters or if you're tired of your own content. Try out different things, such as different types of subject lines, different layouts, and different content. Changing things up isn't a bad thing unless every newsletter you're sending out is a screaming success. Research what others are doing that people seem to like and put those things to use. A newsletter doesn't have to be a huge stressor. Instead, it can be like a conversation with your subscribers. You can even put questions in it, such as what people most enjoyed and what they'd like to see in future newsletters. Bear in mind that nobody will have a 100% open or click-through rate, so don't get disappointed if you don't. Believe it or not, 20% is considered a good open rate. Set goals for your open rate and try things out until you meet those goals. Above all, try to make it interesting and engaging.

CHAPTER SUMMARY

- Newsletters are important and beneficial to authors.
- There are several free newsletter sites with varying levels of features.
- Provide various means for people to sign up for your newsletter, including paper sign-ups at in-person events and a form on your website.
- Be ethical about how you add people to your newsletter list. They must have requested to be on the list.
- Offer freebies to encourage people to sign up.
- Pay attention to colors and fonts, making sure the newsletter is easily readable and interesting, but not over-the-top gaudy.
- Have a compelling subject line.
- Provide links to social media, your website, your publications, and any events you're doing.

CHAPTER 25
CLAIMING PAGES ON VARIOUS BOOK OUTLETS

There are several sites where it's helpful, if not vital, to claim your account and have a presence. The three big ones are Amazon, Goodreads, and Bookbub. This is true even if you have no solo titles out, though in that case it's most important to be on Amazon and Goodreads.

AMAZON

Amazon is the major one and should be the first one you sign up for, at least if any title you're in is for sale through them. Having an account with AC means you'll have a searchable name and a profile landing page that includes a headshot, a listing of your books, and a bio, plus readers will be able to follow your account in order to get updates. There are additional extras, such as being able to link your blog to your AC account so that each new post shows up with a preview and a link on your profile. For those who choose to self-publish via Amazon in the future, this will be where sales numbers and ranks can be tracked, which will come in handy.

In order to create this account, go to authorcentral.amazon.com. You'll want to bookmark this in order to maneuver back in the future.

There's a button right on that page that says "Join Now." Click on this and either link it to your Amazon purchasing account you already have or create a completely new account. You'll want it to be under the name you publish under most frequently. You'll be able to add aliases and such later. If you have a separate author email, which you should, and your regular Amazon purchasing account is under a different one, it will behoove you to start a new one instead of linking the two accounts. I didn't do this, and it means all my author updates, such as royalties, go to my personal email instead of my author email, and it drives me nuts. However, fixing it after the fact is a much bigger pain, so I've stuck with it.

The rest of it is pretty self-explanatory. Fill out the information requested. Make sure it's a landing page that looks professional and that you'll want everyone looking at your books or stories to have access to. Unless it's changed, there must be one title minimum that you can claim in order to finish setting up this account, whether it's something you've self-published or a traditionally published piece. It's a great victory lap after a first publication to be able to go in, claim a book, and set up an author account on Amazon. People often ask how they can find your books when you're an author; being able to say they can plug your name into the Amazon search bar and find you feels amazing. To claim a book, which gets your name and a link to your author profile, there's an item in the menu on your AC page that allows you to claim a book. Once you click to do so, a search bar will appear. Plug the book title in here and search until you find the correct book. It will give you several categories for why you're claiming the book, including one that says you're one of many authors on a title. Choose the correct category and give them whatever evidence they need. Most commonly, the book description on the book page will list all the involved authors. In the field asking how you can prove you're part of this book, simply put a note that your name is in the book description. This will be confirmed, then you'll get an email saying they've confirmed and approved it. Within a couple days, you'll be able to go to the book page and see your name. Now you're official!

The publisher of an anthology has a limit on how many author names they can enter, which means not everyone in an anthology will be in that top line leading to author accounts. This means you'll have to manually claim titles you're in sometimes using the same method from the last paragraph here. Though it won't add your name to the very top under the title, anyone scrolling down will be able to find your name and headshot down the page. Other types of proof that you're part of a book can include linking to the publisher website, author names on the book cover image, and a table of contents visible in the preview feature.

Someone visiting your author page, which they can do by clicking on your name on any relevant book page or by searching your name and clicking on the author account, will be able to see all your claimed books and easily buy something else from under your name. It also means that someone liking your story in an anthology will be able to find your solo books if and when you have them available. One warning here is that the more the books sell, and the more reviews there are, the more searchable your name will be. The way the algorithms work, even if you have several books available, if they aren't selling rapidly you will be moved down in their algorithms. This problem has gotten worse for Indie authors in recent years, making it so your name may be several pages in on the search feature, so encourage those reviews and ratings in order to bump up your books. This isn't an issue for you personally until you have solo books or short stories out, but it's good to be aware of when that time approaches.

Amazon does offer ads, which will appear as book recommendations on searches and on product pages. You can set a budget for how much total you're willing to spend on the ads, then put in bids for what you're willing to pay per click. This can be tried out with a lower budget to test how it works for you. If it isn't working, something may need to be tweaked. Ads are only a good idea for you if you have a solo book out and even Amazon admits in their information that it works best for books that are already getting some attention and favorable reviews. It's something worth looking into and trying, though, considering the low cost with which you can start.

Screen grab of my Amazon author page

GOODREADS

The next one we'll go over is Goodreads. Goodreads is a site that is very much more for readers than writers. However, it's still important to claim your account so you can personalize the author page here. As with Amazon, you can tie your blog in so that there's something actively updating on the author page. It's also possible to run give-aways and such from the platform. Your readers are able to ask questions, which you'll be notified about by email, and it can be quite fun answering those. Those questions and answers will then remain on the author page until enough others are asked to move them off.

To claim your author account, go to goodreads.com and create an account. Again, be sure to do this under your author name and email. You will then search for a book you're in, where you should find your name if it was put in by the publisher. Click on your name, which will take you to the generic profile page, and on the bottom of the page you can click where it says "Is this you? Let us know!" There will be information to fill out and submit, and then you'll be notified by email when you've successfully claimed your account. Then you can go in and fill in your profile.

It's a little trickier to claim a book on Goodreads than it is on Amazon. To do so, you have to go to the Goodreads Librarians Group, where there's a forum. One category under the forum is "Adding New Books." You have to start a thread on the forum with your information and the book's title and/or ISBN and ask the Librarians to add the book to your account. They typically do it pretty fast. Bookmarking this forum would be a good idea, as would bookmarking your author profile.

Goodreads offers ads like Amazon, but they also offer a giveaway option. Authors can sign up to either give away up to 100 e-books or a smaller number of print books. There is a cost involved, and it's not inexpensive. Their pages says giveaways start at $119 for a campaign, so this probably makes sense for someone with a higher advertising budget and some other solo books already out. It seems odd to have to pay to give free copies of your book to people when there are surely better ways to do so. For example, if you self-publish your e-book via Smashwords, they allow you to give coupons for no cost, and you can modify your prices whenever you like. The short version here is that I'm not a big proponent of Goodreads promotions, but I'd be remiss if I didn't tell you they existed. As with Amazon, should you choose to do paid promotions through them, it would not be a good idea for anthologies in which you have stories, only for your own solo collections.

Screen grab of my Goodreads author page

BOOKBUB

The third platform is BookBub. BookBub is especially handy upon a release of a new book, because it will send an automated email out to anyone following your author account to let them know you have a new release. To claim your author account, go to bookbub.com/partners/free_tools. Scroll to the bottom of this page and click on "Sign Up Free." It will lead to a set of questions, starting with asking what your role is. Choose "Author" or you won't be able to claim your author account. Follow the directions from there until you've claimed your account. Once you've completed all steps, it's just a matter of waiting for the email confirming you've gotten your account. At that point, you can sign in and set up your profile.

While BookBub does automatically add books to your profile that have your name on them, always check to be sure they've been successfully added. Otherwise, you'll have to manually claim your book. To do so, go into your author profile and click "My Books." This will bring up a list of your books, and there will be a button at the top that says "Add Book." Here, you'll enter the title into a search bar and choose the correct book to add. After the initial signing up, BookBub is pretty simple to use. Look around the account to see what you can do with your account, including promotions.

Currently, BookBub is considered the strongest in terms of ads for new authors' books. Be sure to research your audience and comparable independent authors so you can target the ads accordingly should you want to try them. BookBub allows those with few or no followers to target the readers of other authors, and they recommend you use other independent authors, rather than more famous traditionally published authors. Their two main plans are for launching a new book or advertising a deal or discount. As they explain on their promotions page, ads for already released books tend to work best when they're advertising a special, lower price. As far as launches, any followers you already have on the platform will get notified once your book releases. If you want to send news of an available pre-order, there will be a cost associated. Just as with the other platforms, paid promotions only make sense for your solo books, not for anthologies you're part of.

Screen grab of my BookBub author account

REVIEWS

It's important that you never respond to reviews on your books. Even if yours is one story in an anthology, your story may get singled out. Usually, it's a good thing, with a story being called out if it was better than its counterparts, but there is a chance it could be mentioned in a negative light. Some authors refuse to look at their reviews. I mostly stay away from mine, but I have weak days where I go check. Others check them regularly. If you're in an anthology and the editor is good about checking the reviews, they'll usually let you know if your story was singled out in a good way, which can give you quite a boost in confidence. It's up to you how much you check your reviews, but never ever respond and never argue. It will only make you look bad, and it won't redeem your story in any way. This includes responding to positive reviews. Don't do it. Let the warmth rush over you, save the review if you want to, but don't respond even to say thank you.

CONCLUSION

While there are other accounts like these, the three mentioned here are the primary ones at this time. It's a good idea to sign up for these author accounts as soon as you have one book to claim, which can be an anthology you have a single story in. While updating each of these when you have a new release will take a bit of time, they're pretty easy to do and it's not a constant thing like social media is. Plus, they help get the word out to your readers in various ways and offer differing levels of promotion for each. It's ultimately worth it to have that presence and to research all the options to help get the word out when you have a new release.

CHAPTER SUMMARY

- It's a good idea to create an author account and claim any books you're in as soon as you have at least one title out, even if that's an anthology in which you have one story.
- You will have to prove you're in an anthology, but it's usually easy to do.
- If you have solo collections out, Amazon, Goodreads, and BookBub all have ways in which to pay to promote your book.
- Never respond to reviews on your books or stories, whether they're good or bad.

CHAPTER 26
HEADSHOTS

While a headshot itself is not necessarily what you'd consider marketing, it's instrumental in many of the marketing aspects. People connect more with someone who has a face, versus just an image. And the further you get in your career, the more there's an expectation of professionalism. Conferences and publications will expect their authors to have professional headshots. Sure, you see plenty of candids and selfies, but you probably notice they're exactly that, rather than a professional headshot. As someone who has worked in conferences and running events, I can say that the staff definitely notice, and there are always people who send some awful, blurry photo that will be on a page alongside professional photos. Sadly, those really stand out to people looking up faculty or speaker information.

Most of us don't like having our photos taken, but it's fairly easy to do and will make a difference. Plus, they'll last for quite a while, though some recommend getting a new headshot annually. That seems to be overkill, but getting a new headshot every few years if you're active as a speaker or making appearances isn't a bad idea. Or if you make a drastic change to your appearance.

It's a good idea to find a photographer who is familiar with headshots. There are plenty of other careers that require some sort of professional photo, and there should always be a photographer who feels comfortable taking one. Do your research and look up their gallery, if they have one, to see if there are any professional photos. You can always ask for referrals from other authors. There may also be reviews available online for photographers you're looking at, so check those out, as well. Something that's become more common at professional writing conferences is having a photographer taking bookings over the course of the conference to do headshots. These are usually quite reasonably priced, and it's convenient since you're already at a conference and likely dressing somewhat professionally in the first place.

Once you've decided on a photographer, talk to them about the following:

- Locations for the photoshoot
- Backgrounds
- Outfits and how many changes they'll allow
- What type of editing they offer
- Pricing
- How many photos they'll provide
- The rights they'll give you (a headshot does you no good if you can't use it—get a license or the rights in writing)
- Whether they print the photos and how they'll get the prints and/or digital images to you
- When they'll get the photos to you

A good photographer is going to make you feel comfortable and walk you through the process. You should also take into consideration your author persona and the genres in which you write. For example, I have a regular headshot that looks professional, but I also have a couple fun horror-themed ones I can use for horror publications. Having choices means I can gear my headshot for whatever use I have for it. If I wrote primarily humor, I'd definitely want to gear at least one headshot toward that theme. Your headshot will express whatever you're intending to express as long as you plan it out, take everything under consideration, and convey it to the photographer. Any photographer worth their salt should be able to work with you to get the valid themes out of the photos.

Try to get plenty of sleep the night before your photoshoot. It's also a good idea to set the photoshoot for when you're at your most awake and energetic, because you should also *look* like you're awake and energetic then. This means that if you're a night person you should set up the photoshoot for late afternoon or early evening. If you're a morning person, get them taken in the morning. Of course, if you're doing an outdoor photo shoot, the lighting will be the most important part, and the appointment would need to be scheduled around that, as well. It's also recommended that you be nicely hydrated.

In terms of what to wear, there are quite a few nit-picks when you do your research. One tip is to know what colors work with your skin tone. If you're not sure, ask friends, look through old photos of you, or consult an expert, such as someone at a salon who does makeovers. Avoid strong patterns, because they're distracting, and don't wear jewelry that will steal the photo or overpower your face. The attention should go to your face, whether you want it to or not. That's what engages those looking at the headshot.

A tip I discovered when researching for my first photoshoot was that it was actually a bad idea to look sexy, even if you're a romance author. This extends to not having a lot of cleavage in a picture and overdoing makeup. It has been found to turn off readers, and you're trying to draw them in with your headshots. Another thing that surprised me, as someone with naturally curly hair, is that you shouldn't have curly hair in the photo. If you do stick with your natural curls, they should be neatly done. When I spoke to a professional hairdresser friend who worked for a news station she agreed that it's discouraged, because unfortunately curly hair can convey a messiness in photos, whether it's true or not. Though the obstinate part of me wanted to go with my natural curls as an act of rebellion, I did ultimately get my hair straightened, and I'm happy with how my photos turned out.

I opted to get my hair professionally done ahead of time, which took a bit of stress off my plate. There is also the option of getting makeup professionally done beforehand. Makeup is necessary in headshots for women, and sometimes men, but it should not be overdone or overly dramatic. Again, you're shooting for professional, not vampy. Stage makeup is not necessary, as a good photographer will be working with good lighting, but is also much closer than an audience to a stage. If you're not good at covering blemishes and imperfections, you can discuss those being edited after the fact.

Speaking of which, discuss your editing expectations with your photographer. You don't want to be overedited to the point of looking fake. However, there may be something you'd like edited, such as that stress zit that broke out the night before your photoshoot. While I had good skin the first time I got headshots, I've aged since then. My next photoshoot will probably involve a little removal of blemishes and imperfections. Some photographers will give you an opportunity to ask for additional edits after their first edit run-through, so it's good to know ahead of time what will be allowed and how much say you'll have.

Finally, it's important to be as comfortable and relaxed as possible. While this is easier said than done, discomfort will come across in the photos. Comfort lends itself to confidence, which will also show through in photos. However you're being posed, try to find a way to be physically comfortable with it. If you're in a ridiculous pose that hurts to be in, it's likely not going to look great for your headshot. Take a couple minutes to chat with the photographer at the beginning of the shoot to help feel more comfortable and relaxed. Take deep, relaxing breaths (don't hyperventilate). Try to smile at your own comfort level, rather than putting on a big fake smile that will come across as fake to people viewing the photo. If you're not a big grinner, don't grin in the photo. If you're a half-smiler like me, then do what you're comfortable with. And if smiles are a huge challenge for you, there's no reason a professional photo has to have a big smile in it, as long as you don't look angry or unfriendly in the photo. In that case, focus on looking open and friendly, rather than stoic and grouchy. Tyra Banks would tell you to Smeyes (smile with your eyes).

CHAPTER SUMMARY

- A headshot is a good idea to have early on, as anthologies sometimes feature photos of the authors. Eventually, you'll need them for appearances.
- Find a photographer who's familiar with headshots.
- Discuss important details with the photographer ahead of the shoot.
- Get rest, hydrate, do your makeup, and dress professionally.
- Consider getting hair and makeup professionally done.

CHAPTER 27
EVENTS AND APPEARANCES

As authors, it's surprising how much appearances can factor into our careers. From fan cons to writing conferences to workshops, readings, podcasts, and online appearances, there are many opportunities to appear as an author. This is where hand selling abilities can come in handy. As a short story author, many of the anthologies offer discounts to their authors, charging them only the cover charge or base cost of the book printing, plus shipping. This means that you can get discounted copies and sell them at events, keeping the overage above the cover charge you paid. It's another way to get some income out of something you most likely got a flat fee or royalty payment from.

WRITER'S CONFERENCES

One big area for appearances is a writer's conference. Most of these conferences now have online applications to propose workshops you'd be willing to teach. This is where outside abilities, such as being an attorney and having insight into the legalities of writing, can benefit you and maybe sell more books. Make sure you pitch workshops you feel confident you can teach. The more knowledgeable you are, the less you have to rely on notes or cards. Establishing your expertise and giving a solid workshop can lead to future invitations at other conferences and events. Try to pitch as many workshops as possible. This will increase your chances of being picked up as a speaker. The reason for this is that most conferences will give speakers free entry to the conference as a trade for appearing. This may be in addition or instead of an actual honorarium, which is the flat fee paid out to a speaker. If they're going to give a free conference to someone, which is not at all free to them as there are associated costs for each guest, they expect that person to be doing a solid amount of work, which means they want someone who can present multiple workshops, not just one.

Most conferences also have a means to sell the faculty's books, usually on a consignment basis if you're not traditionally published in a book that's available through Ingram. For consignment, you bring copies of your book, fill out a form, and hand those copies over. At the end of the conference, you pick up the remaining books and are usually mailed a check for any money brought in. The bookstore at the conference typically takes a small percentage—usually ten-to-fifteen percent—but that information will be disclosed at the beginning on the contract you fill out. Professional conferences typically send the form out to their speakers in advance so they can have plenty of time to review the terms and agree to them.

Conferences are more professional in appearance and activities than conventions, so I recommend wearing business casual to them. They're exhausting and make for long days, so unless you're determined to wear high heels or nice, but uncomfortable, shoes it's best to wear comfortable shoes. If you're pitching to an agent or editor or teaching workshops at a conference, it's a good idea to keep a nicer pair of shoes to change into before these appearances, but to wear more comfortable shoes the rest of the time. If it's a conference you've traveled to, you likely have a room in the same hotel as the conference, which makes it much easier to shoot upstairs and change shoes between appearances. If it's in the city where you live, it becomes trickier, and will likely involve either keeping a spare pair of shoes in your vehicle or carrying around a bag that has the shoes in it.

If you're teaching a workshop, doing a book signing, or having any other sort of appearance, make sure you're dressed well, preferably in that business casual attire, but do try to make it comfortable, as well. If it fits into your comfort zone, even better. Try to have visuals and/or giveaway items, such as business cards, bookmarks, or other novelties. If you do a PowerPoint of your workshop, stick your website and major social media links on the last slide. This is also a good place to include cover images of your books. Having your website on the slide lets people know where to go to find your book, and having that visual of the cover on the slide makes it easy to find.

Practicing the workshop along with the slides is a good idea, because conferences are closely scheduled. There is typically a moderator of some sort whose job is to introduce you and keep you on time. Running over your time, which is typically fifty to sixty minutes unless otherwise specified, especially when it involves ignoring the moderator, is a bad look. It's unprofessional, and it can cause the next speaker to have to start late, robbing them of their full time to finish their workshop on time. For those moderators with the most experience, they're going to ensure you end on time. That may mean you don't get to finish your presentation, which also looks unprofessional and leaves your audience without the closure a conclusion brings.

Make sure you're responsive to the conference staff in the months and weeks leading up to the conference. There will be a varying number of emails with them, including the final choosing of workshops you'll be presenting, the schedule, hotel arrangements, a request for your bio and headshot if it wasn't put in with the proposal, and a request for you to register. Professional conferences try to keep their contacting of speakers to a reasonable minimum, so a lot of these things will be done at once, if possible. There are often speakers who are a pain, who don't respond to emails, don't respond to questions, and in general act like they're above the staff trying to reach them. This isn't a good look, and it will be remembered. While the staff will still act professionally, it can benefit you to already have set up a good rapport between you when you head in. It makes them more likely to help you whenever possible and to make sure you're aware of any extras. It's also important to meet any deadlines they give you, as there are a billion other things they can't complete until each step is finished.

They may also need to get things like handouts from you if you're doing them or your PowerPoint slides if it's an online appearance and they need to preload them. Be sure to get these to them by the deadlines.

Be sure to comport yourself professionally throughout the conference, too. Even if you're solely an attendee and not a speaker, there will be a ton of networking and people may still look up your books. In fact, the top topic of discussion upon first meeting another writer is, "What do you write?" Believe me, you'll hear it a lot. Behaving as a professional can only benefit you moving forward.

A SIDE NOTE ON BAR CON

Bar Con is when the staff, faculty, and attendees hit the bar after a long day at the conference and let loose. Don't get sloppy drunk, and don't get so drunk that you can't control what you say or do. People *will* remember how you acted. However, this is an excellent time to network, as are the meals if they're conference provided versus everyone scattering to find restaurants. This is a good time to chat with that agent you might be interested in for a book. However, do *not* try to sell to them during this time. If they're interested in hearing your pitch, they'll ask for it. Otherwise, you should be focusing on getting to know them and hoping they get to know you, too. That way, should you query them in the future, you can mention that great conversation you had about French bulldogs at that conference, and they might remember you, hopefully fondly.

GREEN ROOM

Professional conferences will usually have a room designated for only the faculty and maybe the staff. This room is meant to be a place the speakers and staff can unwind without having to deal with attendees asking questions or trying to sell agents and editors. If you're a speaker at a conference you'll have access to the green room. It's important that you respect any rules laid out. In addition, there are unspoken rules, such as not fangirling/boying heavily over anyone and not attempting to pitch a book to an agent or editor. While in the green room, you may find yourself face to face with an author you highly respect. You may be overcome with the urge to jump up and down and scream or do something similarly humiliating. Resist. If they're in the green room, that is their safe zone, just as it's intended to be yours. If you must fan over them, do it in the general conference areas or even at Bar Con. As far as editors and agents, absolutely don't pitch to them in the green room unless they say you can. Depending on the conference, you may be discouraged from doing it outside of a scheduled pitch session. Pay attention to the rules outside the green room, too. Irritating an editor or agent is certainly not going to inspire them to publish your book. Given, with short story writers that might not be an issue, but it needs to be stated, just in case.

CONVENTIONS

Conventions are a little looser. At these, it's typically panels, rather than workshops. While a workshop is a single speaker, a panel usually involves up to five people answering questions from a moderator and the attendees in the room. It's harder to prepare for this one, but a lot easier than teaching an hour-long workshop. I typically brainstorm a few questions in advance to both have somewhat prepared answers, but also in case a moderator doesn't show up or no questions are forthcoming from the audience. I've rarely had to use these, but being prepared relieves a lot of my tension and allows me to be more relaxed. Being on panels is a great way to meet other writers, and the more relaxed you are, the better you can roll with the questions that come your way.

While you still need to be a professional (I know, you're probably really tired of that word by now), the dress for cons can be more relaxed in most cases. If you've never been to the con and don't know how most people dress for it, it's probably a good idea to default to business casual. However, if you've been to a convention, such as a Comic Con, and you know the speakers are less formal, dress fun for the con. For me, it's typically jeans and horror-related t-shirts. If you're someone who likes to cosplay, go for it! Just be sure that your cosplay doesn't involve large pieces that take up a ton of room and might inter-fere with fellow panelists who are trapped behind a table with you. Also, be sure to not wear something that might cover your face and make it hard for people to hear you. Not all cons will have micro-phones, so you may be speaking to a large room without a mic. Having that further muffled means your appearance is likely going to be wasted in terms of book sales. People impressed by you are more likely to seek out your books.

One thing to be aware of is that book sales tend to be less at conventions than at writing conferences where you're speaking. You can do twenty panels and still probably not sell as many books at the convention as at a writing conference where you did one workshop. Conventions will not always have a book signing time, and they usually don't have a bookstore. Instead, they charge for table rentals, so the authors selling books are the ones who've paid for a table that they sit at throughout the conference in order to sell their books. The size of the con and where they place the authors can greatly impact the sales numbers, as can the relevance of the books and their genres to the convention itself. For example, as a horror author the timing of the convention and whether there's any sort of emphasis on horror at the con greatly impacts whether I sell books during any book signing times. This would be true if I rented a table, too. Obviously, October is a good month for sales when the books are horror, so October-based events will usually result in better sales for me. If the emphasis at a convention is on science fiction and fantasy, horror isn't going to sell well. These are things that need to be taken into consideration. However, conventions are also usually cheaper than professional conferences, so can be worthwhile more for networking than book sales.

One thing about conventions versus conferences is that you can set up all kinds of things in front of you at the panel table that you might not be encouraged to do at a conference. Have some small, easy to carry bookstands and a copy of a couple of the books you're in (or, later on, your own books). You can set these up in front of the micro-phone or at the front of the table if there's no mic. This is also a good place to put any business cards, bookmarks, or other giveaway items.

Make sure you do not encroach on your neighbors' space. On panels, you're all crammed behind a table together, and you need to be sure to respect everyone else's space, whether they're putting things up or not. Having your books in front of you is a nice way to passively advertise them without being too pushy or in their face. I've actually sold more books out of my bag in the hallway after a panel than I have in any formal signing at a convention. So having them up there tells people you've got books available, and if they're comfortable doing so, they'll approach you. Every book sale is a win, but so is every time a person walks up to the table and takes your card or a bookmark. For a lot of author appearances, it's more about those small steps than any colossal book sales income.

OTHER EVENTS

There are many other kinds of events. Libraries often put on author events intended to connect readers and writers, but also to hold classes for aspiring authors. Be sure to check out your local library to see if there are any opportunities you can apply for. If there are local writer's groups, they're often seeking speakers for various events. It's not uncommon for a writer's group to have some sort of monthly or quarterly programming. For these, you can look on their websites to see if they mention how to propose workshops. Attending some of their events is also a good way to get to know the people running them, so they might consider you in the future. Writer's groups will also sometimes put on group book signings that you can sign up for, so it's a good idea to follow their social media in order to be alerted for sign up invitations. These will consist of you providing your own books via consignment, and will also involve them taking a percentage. Note that events held at libraries that are not sponsored by the libraries themselves frequently don't allow for book sales at all, so in these cases it will be important to have some sort of personal advertising, such as bookmarks or business cards.

There might also be opportunities for readings, meaning you read a portion of one of your stories or the whole thing, depending upon the time limit they put on you. Note that you should only read stories of yours that have already been published unless you're prepared to forfeit selling First Audio Rights for a story. For readings, always be sure to do a read-through or two ahead of time so you know that you're meeting the requested time limit. Bear in mind that you're most likely to talk faster in front of a crowd of people than alone in a room, which also has bearing on workshops you're presenting. Though for workshops you also have to factor in people wanting to ask questions. At least for readings no one is interrupting you.

Podcasts have experienced a boom and are another place you can be a guest. While you can't hand sell books if it's just your voice online, you can still make it a point to direct people to your website. Any podcast that has you on should give you an opportunity to get your information out there for people to find you. That is, after all, the point. Look around for podcasts that discuss your genre or are otherwise relevant to you and see if there are means of contacting them to propose being a guest. Be prepared with what you might have expertise on or be able to speak competently and engagingly about. You're more likely to be a guest if you can tell them why you'd make a good guest. Bear in mind that podcasters that don't focus on writers might still welcome a writer on, so don't exclude those. Especially if there's one you listen to that you think you could be a good guest on. Someone's more likely to invite you on if you let them know you're a listener.

APPEARANCE KIT

Now that I've briefly covered some reasons you might be making an appearance, let's talk about some things you can do to be prepared for them in the future. It's helpful to have some sort of rolling cart so you're not hefting a heavy box around. Try to only bring what fits in the cart, if at all possible, except possibly for posters. There are some great rolling carts available at office stores and home renovation places like Home Depot and Lowes. Keeping the cart packed for the most part means not forgetting something important at a future appearance.

Items to consider having in your appearance kit include:

- Your sales tax licenses (we'll discuss those in a moment)
- Your credit card reader/machine (we'll discuss those, too)
- A newsletter sign-up sheet
- Your business cards (yep, going to talk about these)
- Bookmarks
- Chocolates
- Hand sanitizer
- Tissues
- A small mirror
- Hand lotion
- Lip balm
- Copies of your books
- Book stands
- A tablecloth
- Pens
- A stylus (for credit card purchases)
- Mints or mouthwash
- A brush
- An extra hair clip
- A comfortable pair of slip-on shoes for before and after the event if it's a long one and you're wearing heels.

Any other swag or small decorations can be in the cart, as well, depending upon how much space you have at the event. If you have some sort of large advertisement, there are convenient, foldable easels that might fit in the cart. Otherwise, you might have to carry these separately. Having a simple laptop bag is a good idea for presentations where you'll be doing a PowerPoint, unless your laptop will fit safely into your rolling cart. Having a separate thumb drive with the presentation on it is also a good idea in case there are technical issues with the setup at the venue. You might not be able to use your own laptop, and it sucks to not be able to use the prepared presentation. It's happened to me. Luckily, audiences very much want the speakers to succeed, and they'll support you through it, but no one wants to be in that situation to begin with. Another item it's handy to have is a remote that you can use to advance your slides on the PowerPoint.

Don't depend upon the venue to provide that. These are inexpensive and easy to use. They can be found at office supply stores or online.

When making appearances where you'll be provided with a table to yourself or a shared table, it's nice to have a tablecloth. It shows you were prepared, and your table will be one of the better looking ones. A genre-themed tablecloth can be fun, but a simple tablecloth is nice for more professional appearances. The less intricate your decorations, the better, because you want it to be fairly easy to set up your table. The chocolates I mentioned for the kit are handy. People love free candy. You can choose what you want to hand out. It doesn't even have to be chocolate, but I've found that's the most popular. I usually put out a couple non-chocolate pieces, too, for those who aren't chocoholics. For the newsletter sign-up sheet, I take a clipboard to keep it neat. The fields on the sheet ask for the person's name and their email address. An alternative to a sign-up sheet is having a tablet where they can sign up for the newsletter digitally. Either way works.

BUSINESS CARDS AND BOOKMARKS

For the business cards and bookmarks, both of these are handy to have. The business cards are something you can have as soon as you have a website to refer people to. They can come in handy at networking events, not just for readers but for fellow writers, agents, and editors you meet. I've talked to people at conferences who invited me to submit a story to them, and in order to get in touch with each other we've exchanged business cards. It's a good idea to have them, just in case. In addition, if you keep some in the wallet or purse you usually carry around, you may run into someone any time, at the supermarket or a café, who might want to know how to find your books. While the opportunities to exchange business cards may not be frequent, it's best to be prepared for the possibility. In addition, as mentioned before, they're good to have at any appearances so people wanting to know more about you and your books can find you.

Bookmarks are something that come more into play once you have a solo collection versus when you're selling anthologies you've placed a story in. If you're at that point, it's a good idea for the business cards and bookmarks to both have cover images on them. You can gear the bookmark to a single book of yours or have multiple images, but a single book tends to be a good idea. A good way to figure out what you might like and to get ideas is to walk around at any event and collect cards and bookmarks from others to see what they're doing. We readers can never have too many bookmarks. Plus, it's research.

SALES TAX LICENSE

Something to be aware of is that any event that allows you to sell your own books and collect payment on your own will require a sales tax license. You should get the required sales tax licenses by default as soon as you have something to sell. Typically, a city and a state sales tax license are required. It depends upon where you live, so research it online. They tend to make it pretty simple to research and complete, and it can all be done online, though there are mailing options, too. For events in your state, but in a different city from where you hold a sales tax license, there are temporary or event sales tax licenses that can be applied for. Sales tax licenses are only required if you're taking the payments yourself. If the event involves you consigning your books, they're taking care of the sales taxes. It's a lot easier that way and means you don't have to remember to file your sales taxes later. Typically, a more formal event will do consignment, while conventions will usually require you to take on all that work and those related costs. Until you're making over a certain amount, most places will only require an annual filing and paying of these sales taxes. However, once sales are higher, it will be quarterly or even monthly, depending upon local requirements and the amount of income.

CREDIT CARD READER

In the case of selling your own books, it's a good idea to have a credit card machine. Square is the most common, and it's easy to get and to use. To create an account and get the reader, go to squareup.com. They also make it pretty simple, and if you use the platform to record any sales, the handy reports will help you file sales tax at the end of the year or whenever you're required to file and pay. There are many variations on credit card readers, so it can be hard to know what you need. Unless you're a bookstore, there's no need to get the big, complicated machines. The standard widget that plugs into your phone is good enough to start and it's free when you sign up for an account. There is also a chip reader option that is handy, so if you have the funds and willingness to spend them, it's worthwhile to get. It works better for reading the card than the simpler mechanism. The chip reader does need to be charged in advance, but the charge lasts a long time.

There are other card readers and systems available, so I'm by no means saying you have to go with Square. It's simply the reader I'm familiar with, both through my personal sales and through larger events with a writer's group I volunteered with, which included bookstores. Some other choices are PayPal and Stripe. When looking into convenient ways to take credit cards as an author, look up Payment Service Providers (PSPs) instead of merchant accounts. Merchant accounts are services like Clover and Toast, which tend to charge a monthly fee on top of per-transaction fees, and they work with larger point-of-sale (POS) systems like actual cash registers at stores and restaurants. Research your options and choose the reader and program that will work best for your personal needs. You should be able to find people you know who've used one or another in order to ask questions.

Whatever mechanism you use will likely involve your phone. You can plug the widget into your phone and setup your books and pricing in advance, plus put in the necessary sales tax amounts. There is also typically a way to take payments offline in case the wi-fi at the venue is spotty or non-existent. For this, the transaction information will be saved until you connect to wi-fi, at which time it will upload all the information and process the cards. There are also a lot of great features available with different systems, including setting up storefronts for websites and similar extras. Understand that they will be taking a cut of your sales and/or charging transaction and processing fees. When it comes down to it, between processing fees, consignment fees, and the costs of purchasing copies of books, this is not a get-rich-quick scheme. You will at times feel nickel-and-dimed to death. But the true benefits come in the form of hopefully bringing readers back for future stories and books, and those sales will build.

ADDITIONAL TIPS

A big side note on appearances: stand up. If you're physically able to, standing up to speak to people or greet people is more engaging. I've had the opportunity to observe a lot of different people at a bunch of events, and it's the people standing up who talk to the most people and ultimately sell the most books. If you're not able to stand, there are ways to be equally engaging, including possibly positioning yourself in front of or beside the table instead of being seated behind it. The point of standing is to be engaging, so if you'd prefer not to or cannot stand, be sure to be engaging. Meet people's eyes, smile, reach out to shake their hands, nod at them. You want to acknowledge their presence by doing whatever you can comfortably do. Shrinking down behind a table will cause them to walk on by.

Standing can also be a good idea when presenting a workshop. Sometimes the arrangement of the room will make it hard to stand while presenting, and that's okay. However, if you're able to stand to present the workshop without tripping over cables or falling off a platform, it can keep people's attention better. The only place it's really not applicable is when you're on multi-person panels. For those, everyone should remain seated. If you're the only one standing, that's weird. Also, standing when you're required to speak into a microphone is only possible if they have a portable microphone available. If not, stay seated where you can speak into the microphone.

Some events are recorded or the room simply doesn't work for someone not using a microphone. While it can be unpleasant to speak into a microphone, and you may have a great voice that gets to the whole room, it's helpful to bear in mind that audience members who are hard of hearing want to be able to hear you, too, and by refusing to use a microphone when requested, you're isolating these attendees. I bucked using microphones at the beginning, because it was somehow more official, like raising my hand instead of just shouting out an answer while I was in school. Once I had an event where someone was struggling to hear, it hit home for me. I want everyone included, if possible.

Here's another big tip: hydrate. Conferences and conventions try to have water for their speakers and panelists, as well as water in the hallways for attendees. Try to always have water on you, whether it's from the provided means or a water bottle you've brought. Part of this is that it's healthier to stay hydrated and will likely make it easier on you to go through a long appearance or event. The other part, though, is that the weird clicky talking that happens when your mouth or throat are dry is annoying for people to listen to. And when you're nervous, as you most likely will be when in front of people, your mouth dries out. This also happens when you're speaking a lot. Keeping water on you allows you to wet your mouth, but it's also one of the first things they teach you in a good speech class. Having water gives you a way to pause if you need it. Forgot what you were going to say next? Take a moment to scan your notes while drinking from your water bottle. Just need a moment to collect yourself? Take a lovely sip of water. It can come in handy in so many ways if you remember to use it. It does take getting used to, but once you do, it becomes automatic to take that drink of water when you need a second to get it together. It can even work if you're speaking about something that makes you emotional and you want to calm down before proceeding. Water. Who knew it could be such an aid?

Some final tips:

- Limit the decorations on your table to a reasonable amount.
- Limit having a bunch of extra people behind the table with you.
- Try not to keep your food on the table and save snacks for breaks.
- Don't bring stinky snacks or ones that will be messy or loud; don't bring something that might leave seeds or other food in your teeth.
- Be on time. Running early is okay as long as it's not super early, which might interfere with setup. Running late is never a good look.

- Make friends with your neighbors. It will not only make the event easier, but can make it so breaks are possible if you watch each other's tables.
- Limit the use of your phone unless you need it for payments. Staring at a screen when people visit your table is bad form.
- Inexpensive book stands can be helpful for display purposes.
- Display book pricing so people don't have to ask.
- Be careful to keep liquids where they can't spill and ruin your books and swag.
- If you're given forms to fill out ahead of time, try to have them prepared before you arrive. If they ask you to scan and email in advance, do so if you're able.
- Bring a sweater or jacket and try not to dress too warmly. Temperatures vary widely between venues, so you don't want to be roasting or freezing. Dressing in layers helps.
- Don't assume there will be a tablecloth. Unless you have one of your own, know that your legs may be exposed under a table, so don't wear a miniskirt or nasty shoes with the expectation that no one will be able to see them.

This chapter is not meant to cover every facet of appearances or the dynamics of every event. That would be a book unto itself, as so many other topics in this book could be. It's intended to give you an idea of things you can do to get yourself out there more and to possibly sell more books, whether it's now or in the future. In addition, it's great for networking with like-minded people. Writers lead lonely lives. It's beneficial to spend time around others who understand what it's really like. Well intentioned friends and family can never understand everything that goes into what you do. But other writers will. In this way, it's also beneficial to join local writer's groups and attend some of their events, when possible. Sometimes socializing with people who understand what it takes is the only thing keeping you whole and able to keep doing it.

CHAPTER SUMMARY

- You can do appearances and events whether you have short stories in anthologies or have your own collections/books.
- Publishers of anthologies may offer the books at a lower cost to the authors in them, which you can take advantage of to hand sell and make additional money.
- Some possible events are writer's conferences, conventions, library events, podcasts, readings, and writer's group events.
- Act like a professional at any event where you're appearing.
- Rehearse workshops you're teaching.
- Office rolling carts can be a convenient way to lug your items to events.
- Consider keeping a pre-packed appearance kit with helpful items in it.
- Some events may require that you have a sales tax license to sell on your own.
- Consider having a way to process credit cards.
- Have swag, such as bookmarks and business cards.
- Stay hydrated at events.
- Stand up to greet people if you're behind a table.

PART SEVEN
CONCLUSION

CONCLUSION

I've cast a fairly wide net in an attempt to give you as much helpful information as possible. My hope is that you can use this book as an ongoing resource as you move through your writing career. Specifically, I want to see you have success with short stories and to be able to do so without having to struggle through finding your way through the trickier parts that no one talks about. Cast aside what you don't need; it will be here waiting for you should the day come when you do require it.

A lot of the short story world has to do with persistence, common sense, and paying attention. The more you produce, the more you get yourself out there. As writers, we must learn to live in a world full of rejection. It's the small successes that carry us through, whether that's a publication, a positive mention of a story in a review, or the day there are enough stories to bundle into a collection. Every step of the way is full of risk, fear, exhilaration, and excitement. That, and a whole lot of waiting.

With the information from this book under your belt, you should be able to shape your career the way you want to. No more tiptoeing. Make of it what you want. If you want to publish a few stories here and there, go for it. If you want to become a prolific short story writer, do it. If you want to write some short stories in your novel world and use them as rewards for your readers, more power to you. The point of short stories is that they're flexible and can be used in many different ways. They're also great fun. Enjoy your time dabbling. Perhaps you'll decide you want to do more with the art of short stories, after all.

Whatever your mission, I hope you find this book to be a helpful resource. I want every one of you to find success in the writing world.

And don't forget...always read the submission guidelines.

PART EIGHT
RESOURCES

COMMON TERMS

Common terms found in this book and elsewhere:

Acceptance – When a story is purchased by a market.

Anthology – A book collecting stories/poems from multiple authors.

Attribution – Credit to the original creator or publisher of something.

Beta Reader – An individual you ask to read a manuscript and give feedback.

Bio – A short, third-person description of the author.

Blind Submissions – When no information is given on the manuscript to ensure the judges/editors are choosing on the basis of the story, not the names.

Byline – Attribution for wrote the story. This is either your real name or your pen name, depending upon whether you have a pen name.

Collection – A book collecting stories/poems from one author.

Contributor Copy – A free copy, whether electronic or print, given to authors published in that specific book/magazine.

Copyright – Ownership over a story.

Cover Letter – A brief presentation of information about an author and story to be placed in an email along with a submission.

Critique Group – A group put together to read each others' work and give feedback.

Domain Name – A URL, the identifier for a website.

Electronic Rights – Rights over a story to be published electronically (e-book, website).

First North American Serial Rights – Gives a publisher the right to publish a story before anyone else in North America.

Flat Fee – A single payment to an author at a set amount.

Formatting – The details in shaping a manuscript for submission, such as font, double spacing, margins, etc.

Form Rejection – When a generic message is sent with a rejection.

Front Matter – Pages preceding the start of a book, including the title page and copyright.

Genre – The type and style of a story. Where it fits on a bookstore shelf.

Guidelines – Rules that guide how something is done.

Hook – The thing that pulls the reader in. Something compelling or interesting.

ISBN – A number used as an identifier for a published book.

Manuscript – In this book, this refers to a short story manuscript. The completed story.

Market – A magazine or publisher to which you submit stories.

Multiple Submissions – Submitting more than one story (or poem) to a market at once.

Pen Name – Your nom de plume. The name you write under if you prefer not to write under your real name.

Personal Rejection – When a personal note is added to a rejection.

Print Rights – Rights over a story to be published on paper.

Query – In the short story world, an inquiry sent to a market that has not responded to a previously sent submission or an advance email proposing a story idea.

Query Letter – A letter sent to an agent or novel publisher in an attempt to sell them your collection or book.

Reader Magnet – Something free given to readers in an attempt to exchange it for their email address to add to your newsletter. Must be significant, such as a free short story.

Rejection – When a story is turned down by an editor or slush reader.

Reprint – A story that has been published or made available to the public already, and is being submitted to be published for a second time. First rights have already been taken.

Rewrite Request – When a market neither rejects or accepts a story, but sends a request that it be modified/edited within specific parameters.

Rights – Who has what ownership over aspects of a story.

Royalties – When a percentage of ongoing income is paid out to the involved authors.

SASE – Self-Addressed Stamped Envelope

Short Listed – When your story is kept for consideration for a publication. It's considered to be on the short list of finalists.

Shunn Formatting – See SMF.

Simultaneous Submissions – Sending a story to more than one market at a time.

Slush Readers – Typically the first line of people who read short story submissions when they come into a magazine.

SMF – Standard Manuscript Format—the default formatting for submissions when no other instructions are given.

Submission – A short story sent to a market.

Submission Guidelines – Rules and formatting guides to prepare submissions.

Submission Portal – A program used by publishers to take submissions so they aren't sent via email.

Swag – Items to give away with the intention of advertising a book or author.

Synopsis – Summary of a story.

Theme – A unified topic for a group of stories.

Withdrawal – When an author decides to take back a story they've submitted, for whatever reason.

LIST OF RESOURCES

Books

- *On Writing*, Stephen King (just because every writer should read it)
- *Bird by Bird: Some Instructions on Writing and Life*, Anne Lamott
- *Self-Publisher's Legal Handbook*, Helen Sedwick
- *Information in a Nutshell: Business Tips and Taxes for Writers*, Carol Topp, CPA
- *Writer's Market* (authors differ, but most recently by Robert Lee Brewer)

Websites

- The Creative Penn (thecreativepenn.com)
- Writer Nation (thewriternation.com)
- Writers in the Storm (writersinthestormblog.com)
- Jen Friedman (janefriedman.com)
- Writer Beware (accrispin.blogspot.com)

- Insecure Writer's Support Group (insecurewriterssupportgroup.com)
- Writer Unboxed (writerunboxed.com)
- DIY MFA (diymfa.com)
- Duotrope (Duotrope.com)
- Submission Grinder (thegrinder.diabolicalplots.com)
- Classic Short Stories (classicshorts.com)
- American Literature – 20 Great American Short Stories (americanliterature.com/twenty-great-american-short-stories)
- Ralan (ralan.com)
- Published to Death (publishedtodeath.blogspot.com)
- Horror Tree (horrortree.com)
- William Shunn (for formatting) (shunn.net/format)
- Query Tracker (querytracker.com)
- Publishers Marketplace (publishersmarketplace.com)
- Who Unfollowed Me (who.unfollowed.me)
- Bowker (myidentifiers.com)
- Books 2 Read (books2read.com)
- Chrys Fey (writewithfey.com)

HASHTAGS FOR WRITERS

TWITTER

#AmWriting – Tweet about things coming up while you write

#AmReading – Tweet what you're currently reading

#MSWL – Manuscript Wishlist – Search on this to find what agents/editors are seeking

#1K1H – Tweet to challenge others to write 1000 words in 1 hour with you

#1LineWednesday – Tweet a line from your work in progress on a Wednesday

#AmEditing – Tweet about your editing frustrations

#AuthorChat – Use to chat with other authors

#AskEditor – Ask editors a question

#AskAgent – Ask agents a question

#AskAuthor – Ask authors a question

#BookGiveaway – Use if you want to do a giveaway

#FollowFriday/#FF – Use to recommend Twitter accounts for others to follow

#FridayRead – Tweet what you're reading on a Friday

#ShortStory – Tweet about experiences writing short stories, the good and the bad

#WriteGoal – Set a goal before you sit down to write and tweet it out; reply to follow up later

#WriterWednesday/#WW – Use this on a Wednesday to connect with fellow writers

#WordCount – Tweet your progress via your word count

#WritersLife – Tweet about the things that happen in your daily writing life

#SelfPublishing – Tweet about self-publishing experiences and connect with other self-publishers

#WritingSprint – Tweet out an invite to do a writing sprint for x period of time

#TeaserTuesday – Post a snippet from your work in progress on a Tuesday

INSTAGRAM

#writersofinstagram/#writersofig/#authorsofinstagram/#authorsofig – Connect with other writers

#writingcommunity/#writingcommunityofig/#writingcommuni-tyofinstagram – Connect with other writers

#indieauthor/#indieauthorsofinstagram – Connect with fellow independent authors

#ASMSG – Stands for Authors Social Media Support Group

#shelfie – Post a photo of your bookshelves

#authorlife/#writerslife – Post photos of your writing life and connect with fellow authors

#bookstagram – Sharing books you're reading or your books

#amreading – Post what you're reading

#amwriting – Post a photo of writing progress, such as a screenshot or a selfie of you writing somewhere

TIKTOK

#writer – Do a video about your writing or writing life

#writing – Do a video about your writing or writing life

#author – Do a video about your writing or writing life

#writerscommunity / #writingcommunity – Great for connecting with other writers or posting video of meeting up with other writers

#bookworm / #greatreads / #mustread – Do a video about a book you're reading or a book you recommend or about your story / book

#shortstory – Connect with short story readers and writers

#booksandcoffee – Connect with readers

#writinggoals – Talk about your goals, set your goal for the day

#writingproject – What are you working on?

#writinginspiration – Discuss what inspires you or inspire others

#booktok – All about books

ACKNOWLEDGMENTS

A lot goes into writing and producing a book, and while it's largely a solo effort there's also a team involved in various ways.

First, to my family, who deals with the days where I'm so engrossed in writing or editing that they have to basically do a song and dance number to pull me away. Specifically to my husband for keeping things running, making my book covers, and in general being supportive.

To the writing community members who help and support where they can. A super late thank you to Samantha Redstreake Geary for the awesome music and writing pairings you drew me into before I was a published author. I've used her author name so people can check her out. To David R. Slayton for being a calming and supportive presence. To Veronica R. Calisto for her humor. To Kim Olgren for always fighting the good fight. To Kameron Claire for offering to help me learn Vellum even though I stubbornly figured it out myself. To Carina Bissett and Hillary Raque Dodge—without the two of you I would have left the Colorado horror scene two years ago. To Christine Ford for sharing her creative creations with me as a pick-me-up.

Huge thanks go out to my beta readers this time around: Dacia Arnold, Jeff Wood, Jenny Kate, Kari Wolfe, Kathie Scrimgeour, MB Partlow, and Carrie Kalmanowitz.

ABOUT THE AUTHOR

A fan of all things fantastical and frightening, Shannon Lawrence writes primarily horror and fantasy. Her stories can be found in over forty anthologies and magazines, plus her three collections. You can also find her as a co-host of the podcast Mysteries, Monsters, & Mayhem. When she's not writing, she's hiking through the wilds of Colorado and photographing her magnificent surroundings, where, coincidentally, there's always a place to hide a body or birth a monster. Find her at www.thewarriormuse.com or www.mysteriesmonstersmayhem.com.

f facebook.com/thewarriormuse
𝕏 twitter.com/thewarriormuse
◉ instagram.com/thewarriormuse

ALSO BY SHANNON LAWRENCE

Blue Sludge Blues & Other Abominations

Bruised Souls & Other Torments

Happy Ghoulidays